GERMAN LEADERS *of* YESTERDAY *and* TO-DAY

GERMAN LEADERS *of* YESTERDAY *and* TO-DAY

BY

ERIC DOMBROWSKI

Essay Index Reprint Series

BOOKS FOR LIBRARIES PRESS, INC.

FREEPORT, NEW YORK

First Published 1920
Reprinted 1967

CONTENTS

CHAPTER		PAGE
I.	Octavio, Baron Von Seidlitz und Neukirk....	1
II.	Friedrich Ebert	8
III.	Erich Ludendorff	16
IV.	Theodor Wolff	30
V.	Mathias Erzberger	36
VI.	Georg Ledebour	48
VII.	Ernst Von Heydebrand und der Laase	54
VIII.	Alfred Von Tirpitz	60
IX.	Friedrich Naumann	73
X.	Wilhelm II	79
XI.	Clemens Delbrück	92
XII.	Hermann Pachnicke	99
XIII.	Otto Hammann	103
XIV.	Adolph Hoffmann	110
XV.	Hellmut Von Gerlach	119
XVI.	Karl Theodor Helfferich	124
XVII.	Philip Scheidemann	135
XVIII.	Hermann Paasche	141
XIX.	Hans Delbrück	147
XX.	Theobald Von Bethmann-Hollweg	151
XXI.	Minna Cauer	158
XXII.	Paul Lensch	164
XXIII.	Ernst Graf zu Reventlow	169
XXIV.	Georg Michaelis	176
XXV.	Gustav Stresemann	183
XXVI.	Lothar Persius	191
XXVII.	Friedrich Von Payer	198
XXVIII.	Kuno Graf Von Westarp	205
XXIX.	Hugo Haase	210
XXX.	Wilhelm Von Waldow	218
XXXI.	Richard Von Kühlmann	225

CONTENTS

CHAPTER		PAGE
XXXII.	Paul Fuhrmann	231
XXXIII.	Georg Graf Von Hertling	238
XXXIV.	Robert Friedberg	246
XXXV.	Hans Georg Von Beerfelde	252
XXXVI.	Paul Von Hintze	262
XXXVII.	Rosa Luxemburg	271
XXXVIII.	Maximilian Von Baden	277
XXXIX.	Kurt Eisner	285
XL.	Wilhelm Karl Dittmann	294
XLI.	Adolph Groeber	299
XLII.	Emil Eichhorn	304
XLIII.	Karl Liebnecht	310
XLIV.	Walter Adrian Schücking	320
XLV.	Gustav Noske	328

GERMAN LEADERS of YESTERDAY and TO-DAY

I

OCTAVIO, BARON VON ZEDLITZ UND NEUKIRCH

The political activity of Octavio, Baron von Zedlitz und Neukirch, dates back to the time when Prussia consisted of the Rhine provinces, the Altmark, and East Elbia. He was born in Glatz in 1840, the year of Friedrich Wilhelm III's death. His father was president of the Royal Prussian Government. The son arrived at a lesser station in life but nevertheless enjoyed great political influence. He and Prussia grew up together, but at heart he represented the old Prussia. Now that Monarchism, with an audible jerk, turned onto new tracks, Octavio, the knightly old champion, laid his tired body upon the sick-bed. With Hebbel's Master Anton he sighed resignedly:

"I no longer understand the world whose political bumps I have tried to smooth with cunning compromises for so many decades. Now it is everything or nothing, just like the battlefield under cannon fire, equal suffrage or the iron rod. What have I to do with that?

"After all, I have the right to get tired. I have had a turn at every office and have become a political factotum. I still remember passing my state examination for the bar, and that, immediately thereafter, I was sent upon an official mission abroad. Those were years in which the fate of the European continent was gambled for. In 1864 I was appointed to the Prussian Civil Commission in the annexed Duchies of Elbia. Ach! and two years later the merry war with Austria! In Königgrätz they picked up the badly wounded, smart, young, militia officer from the battlefield. Yes. And when I was well again I began slowly, slowly, year by year, to tread the traditional, bureaucratic, seniority march: First assessor, then sheriff in Sagan. Then came a sudden pause. War with France mixed everything in a mess. To be sure, when I think of it, it was but a child's game compared to the present. All at once I was Under-prefect in San Quentin. I wonder if the old house is there? I don't suppose so. The bullets will have razed it to the ground along with all the rest. But what's the difference? Live stock and dead, whole generations are rooted out, stock and branch, and we old fellows have nothing better to do than to lay the rest of our petty existences under the scythe as soon as possible.

"In those days life had just begun for me. Bismarck was building the new nation with broad sweeps and I was permitted to sit in his shadow and help. The district of Sagan-Sprottan sent me to the Reichstag; I took my seat there on the Conservative bench. But I did not belong to the malcontents while the Iron Man was carrying on his liberal policy. He had a fine scent for such things and one day I exchanged my Landsrat office for a post as assistant in the chancelry. My activity in the Reichstag was at an end, and after that I only ran for the Prussian House of Representatives. I was loyal to this from 1876 to the last. Then I entered the Board of Trade. In between lay a long, long, period of parliamentary strivings, fore and aft the wings, always compromising, always welcomed by all parties and members of the Government. I knew the people. I saw kings come and go, systems and tendencies change, ministers and privy councillors, representatives and voters, and, at last, I saw that everything was cooked with water, thin water; the most clever politics were muddied by personal ambitions and material yearnings. I sought for a compromise and they called me Octavio, the Half-dark.

"Gradually I began to like these twilight politics. Especially after Stumm and Kardoff departed this life and I became indisputable tactician at the head of the Free Conservative party. Our party lived on the disunity of the others, but you must not scold me for being a political wash-rag because I and my party were ever ready for compromise. I enjoyed my life as everyone else, liked my beer and loved my wine, was not entirely oblivious to the tender passion. Naturally I have had misfortunes in my private life, too. And you know I have not hidden myself behind the bushes like Adam while the public asked, 'Octavio, where art thou?' It was really a heavy blow to me when my son played that silly, student trick in Leipzig. You remember it was in some wine-room not far from the Bavarian station that he shot his sweetheart, a barmaid, in a fit of jealousy. But, he went to America as correspondent of the *Berliner Anzeiger* and became a good, steady-going fellow who earned his living like everyone else.

"Excuse me, I digress. I was to speak of politics. Where was I? Oh, yes, political wash-rags. That was certainly not my failing. I was just made president of the Sea Board of Trade when that abominable canal project was brought up before the Landtag. The Conservatives were against it. The Kaiser declared in an almost autocratic tone: 'It shall be built!' But the Conservatives would not bend. I was one of those rebels, like Dallwitz, Jagow, and so on, who were pushed out of office by an angry Government. The others rallied long ago and have since become governors, ministers, presidents, and what not. And I? When I reached the age of seventy-five, they gave me the office of Privy Councillor with the title of Excellency. I never reëntered the Government although I had been Bülow's friend and assistant; even Bethmann-Hollweg gladly made use of me, for example at the time of the great reform of the Prussian franchise in 1910, which went so well at first on my compromise recipe, but which failed at the last.

"Believe me, in June, 1917, I had the Right, the Middle, and even the Center party, so far that everyone was almost ready to swear by my pretty plural system plan. Even Bethmann-Hollweg stood godfather and smiled benignly from a discreet distance. And then — he left us in the lurch and proclaimed equal suffrage. I was simply dumbfounded! I couldn't believe it. He had a reliable majority for my plural reform in his pocket, and then to do such a thing! But quickly I got another little compromise ready — and then — then — my own party left me in the lurch! I was too much Left for them in this question. That was the heaviest blow of my life. I decided to resign my seat as leader of the party. Can you possibly imagine what will happen if the House of Representatives is really dissolved? Is it comprehensible? If you please, I still believe in the old conservative dogma, that conservatism and Government are one and the same thing and the only liberality permissible is that the gentlemen of the Government may become Free Conservatives if they wish. All other politics are more or less suspicious, the National Liberals, the Center, the Progressives, the Poles, and the Social Democrats.

They should be regarded only as objects of administration by the Government. At all events, I have participated with beating heart in every exception and have not yet been converted. How often I have sprung upon the speaker's platform when my legs were still steady, with my face red from excitement, my bald head gleaming, and my still stately white beard forming a dignified frame for my words. I was not an orator although I always spoke without notes.

"But I always had the ear of the House. My adjectivity, my rich experience in all branches of Prussian administrative practice overwhelmed them. For the press I was ever the political lexicon. What have I not written about in the red *Tag?* And in the *Post,* the chief organ of the Free Conservatives? I was always the sign-post at every political cross-road. And now that is supposed to be all over. I may not speak, I may not write, I may no longer grope along hidden paths, I may only lie in bed counting over the years of my life, or whatever else the doctor allows. If you look out of the window at Prinz-Albrecht Strasse you will see there, and everywhere else, another sick man whose heart is beginning to falter and whose feet are beginning to swell. His name is Prussia. And the doctor who administers his medicine is Democracy. I suspect Bernard Shaw was not so far wrong when he wrote that satire, *The Doctor's Dilemma.* 'Every doctor

is ten times and a hundred times over a murderer. I would like to think that people and the whole world would suddenly recover if we did away with doctors.'
And perhaps politicians, too!

"Excuse me if I turn over on the other side in disgust."

The old God of the Prussians took pity upon His servant, and when the revolution shook the temple of Prussianism to its very foundation, he said to his tired and bewildered believer, "Get thee hence, son, and join thy forbears, for here is no longer a place for thee!"

II

FRIEDRICH EBERT

I made the acquaintance of Friedrich Ebert at a reception given by the German Society, to which I was invited by Dr. Self, then Secretary of the Colonies. A middle-sized gentleman with a leaning toward corpulency, who makes little of formality; unpretentious, but not laying his innermost soul bare for the crowd to gape at. He is very friendly, very amiable and obliging, but a thin veil separates him from the others. He is one who reflects without brooding, one who is ready to back his words with deeds, to help when necessary; a handworker, a saddler; a master who knows his public and the people; one who has been pushed to the front line of politics by four turbulent years of war, who daily recognizes how little brain matter is applied to so-called world politics. He saw them all come and go, Bethmann-Hollweg, Delbrück, Helfferich, Jagow, Michaelis, Zimmermann, Hertling, and Hintze, people and little people with trembling hands and mysterious countenances, supported by dusty records, gently infusing their political wisdom into the representatives. How many times he was called even late at night, as leader of the

FRIEDRICH EBERT

Social Democrats, to the Chancellor's palace for a consultation with Mr. Chancellor.

And he saw them all, the Government people with the Kaiser at their head — the Kaiser grown so very small before the threatening course of events — saw them wooing the favor of the Social Democrats, this "rabble of rogues without a country." And he thought his own thoughts.

He was born at Heidelberg and existed in the days when all Germany was rejoicing at the victory over France, when flags waved from every house in honor of the new, imperialistic German nation which arose at Versailles. Friedrich grew up without any particular interruption, in humble circumstances, in an almost proletarian narrowness. His father was one of those superfluous men whose gray and sordid lives consist only of work. The mother was like all mothers in narrow streets and crooked courts, shawl on head, old and careworn. Friedrich went to the public school and at fourteen was apprenticed to a saddler. The world about him was so beautiful; the Black Forest, the Neckar, the Ottheinrichsbau, the exuberant students; while he belonged to the "disinherited." He felt himself drawn to the outcasts of society, to the despised ones of the earth. Greedily he devoured the papers, the circulars secretly passed from hand to hand, and while reading and learning he filled his soul with socialistic ideals.

LEADERS OF YESTERDAY AND TO-DAY

Suddenly the bars were down. Bismarck was deprived of office, must leave the Chancellor's palace within a few hours after thirty-eight years of service as president of the Prussian ministry, as Federal and Imperial Chancellor. The Kaiser insisted. He could no longer resist taking the reins of the Government in his own hands. The law against Socialists fell with the Iron Man. The February concessions seemed to introduce a new era. A mental April storm swept the land. Even Ebert was infected. The way was open now, one could work and fight openly for the ideals of Social Democracy.

Friedrich's wander years ended in Bremen; he swam to the top with his fresh, pulsing, southern blood, and became editor of the *Bremer Bürgerzeitung*. Years passed quietly by. He was elected to membership and gradually worked his way up to the secretaryship of the party. Five years later he was president of the Center for Working Youths and a member of the executive committee of the whole party. He looked strange among all those blond and brown comrades. A south German with Roman blood? Perhaps. His temperament was thoughtful and yet energetic when occasion required. He was great at organization, his long suit.

He came into Parliament at the Königsplatz in 1912, with the socialistic wave of that time. He was elected from Elberfeld-Barmen, Scheidemann's neighboring district. Scheidemann and Ebert soon became good friends. When war broke out they both supported the Government and were true to Bethmann-Hollweg for three years. They were not backward in acknowledging the "spirit of August 4th, 1914," when the radicals began to bluster and swagger around the party, nor even when Haase, who was chairman, unrolled the flag of rebellion. Quarrels and scenes took place within their four walls and outside in the forum of the Reichstag. The Labor party split, Haase was dethroned, Ebert, his successor, together with Scheidemann, became the targets for mockery, contumely, and persecution. Members of the party tore each other to pieces publicly. The last bridges to an understanding seemed to be destroyed. The majority of Social Democrats stuck to the Progressives and the Center in order to accomplish any practical, positive work. Ebert, alone, did not give up hope of a reconciliation. In the meantime he became chairman of the all-powerful faction in the Reichstag and presided with a dignity and reserve that won the recognition of his opponents. When the Prince took over the office of Chancellor after the resignation of Hertling, he consulted Ebert; the two understood one another at a time when the catastrophe was no longer to be averted. Ebert was secretary of the first cabinet to be appointed under the parliamentary régime, but he withdrew at the last moment, giving Scheidemann, Bauer and David the preference. The party seemed of more importance to him, the party which was stripped of all her leaders. He waited. Instinctively he felt what was coming.

It came on Thursday, the 7th of November, 1918. The revolutionary movement, beginning at Kiel, spread like lightning all over the nation. Sailors had sent their emissaries to all four points of the wind and the old régime capitulated almost without a struggle. Only the Kaiser, who had left Berlin in time, was hard of hearing. At this moment Prince Max invited Ebert to a conference with him. " I will go to Headquarters this very evening to induce the Kaiser to abdicate," said the Prince. " In that event we can save everything." Ebert, who like Scheidemann had threatened the withdrawal of the party from the Government, now promised to do his utmost to get the party and the masses to wait. But he promised too much. Events were already too far advanced. Almost the whole nation was in revolution; only Berlin was quiet. On the afternoon of the same day, just as the Prince was making ready for the journey, Ebert appeared in the house at Wilhelmstrasse 77, and handed over the ultimatum of the Social Democrats. The die was cast. "That compels me," the Prince answered resignedly, " to hand in my resignation, for it means the overthrow of my policy of persuasion, not force."

FRIEDRICH EBERT

Although the Social Democrats postponed their ultimatum at the last moment, the revolution broke out in Berlin. I still saw the old régime's armored trucks whizzing through the ill-lighted streets on Friday night looking for the "inner foe." After the proclamation of a general strike on Saturday, the 9th of November, I saw the workmen and soldiers marching through the streets unfurling their red flags; I saw them tearing the epaulettes and cockades from their comrades' shoulders; I heard shots, the rattling of machine guns, and I saw Adolph Hoffman and Ledebour making wild speeches in wagons surrounded by a howling throng of youths; I heard Scheidemann's voice from the balcony of the Reichstag building. It was like colored films whizzing past.

Everything seemed a chaos. The only peaceful spot was Ebert. A new era had entered on the wings of a storm. The card house of the old régime had collapsed. The saddler, Friedrich Ebert, lifted the new Germany into the saddle. Sunday morning early newspapers and bill-boards announced Ebert's first manifest: Peace, Freedom, and Order. Coöperation with other parties was made impossible by the resistance of the Independents. Thousands thronged about the Chancellor's palace on Sunday morning. At last the new, purely socialistic Government was born. Six men divided the Chancellor's portfolio: three Social Democrats: Ebert,

Scheidemann, Landsberg; and three Independents: Haase, Dittmann and Barth. Unity had again been established. But hourly new differences arose: arguments with the executive committees of the Workmen and Soldiers' Councils, with the Spartacists, with Liebknecht and Rosa Luxembourg. Ebert held fast to democratic principles and was against any dictation by the proletariat. Those from the other socialistic side were of another opinion. They wished to have at least a part of the socialistic program realized before the National Convention.

The sailors who had placed themselves at the service of the revolution and who had taken up comfortable quarters in the palace, protested against being turned out by the Government. On the day before Christmas eve it became a street fight. "Bloodhound Ebert," screamed the radicals, "shoots down the people." Ebert in dismay capitulated to the marines. Anarchistic radicalism, led by Liebknecht, spread rapidly. It threatened to devour Berlin and all Germany. A new reckoning came. In Berlin the battle lasted seven days. The Ebert-Scheidemann Government battled for its existence and Ebert for his head. The victory was theirs. The election of the National Assembly was accomplished.

And the cabinet laid the portfolio in the hands of the new Parliament.

FRIEDRICH EBERT

When, on February 6, 1919, the National Assembly convened at Weimar, Ebert read the report on the political situation, the house rushed through the adoption of an emergency constitution, and against the votes of the parties of the Right and those of the radical Social Democrats Ebert was elected provisional President of the German Republic. Removed from the stage of parliamentary life, he began, in a quiet and unassuming way, a new activity behind the curtains. Only once he stepped forth again, when during May of the same year the Entente made known the terms of peace. Then he denounced these terms and wanted to resign from office. He lived through hours of doubt and despondency. The Democrats left the Coalition Cabinet in June. The responsibility for fixing the official signatures to the peace document rested alone of all parties with the Centrists and the Majority Socialists. Ebert hesitated, wavered. Should, or should he not, desert his post? But to desert then would simply mean calling in chaos. And so he stayed.

III

ERICH LUDENDORFF

"The General's Tragedy," or "In Disgrace," a film in eight pictures. Paul Wegener as Ludendorff. Music furnished by the Lower Rhine Infantry Band, Regiment 39.

A musical potpourri ushers in the evening. It contains all the patriotic songs "Lieb' Vaterland, magst ruhig sein," "Deutschland, Deutschland über alles," "Was blasen die Trompeten, Husaren heraus!" The overture is over. The room is suddenly darkened. Ludendorff's portrait appears, enormously enlarged, on the canvas. A bulky face. Fleshy and dull. Wrinkles like scars on the façade. A small, stiff mustache hesitatingly adorns the upper lip. The hair flows backward from an imposing brow. It is but a sparse plain. The eyes look defiant, almost gloomy. Personified Will and Ambition veiled in an artificial fog of self-confidence. The picture vanishes as quickly as it appeared. The **real play begins:**

ERICH LUDENDORFF

FIRST PICTURE

Rustling beech forests, calm lakes, and the ocean not far away: Holsteinische, Switzerland. In 1877, at twelve years of age, Erich Ludendorff entered the Cadet school at Plön. He was to enter the fifth class but was found advanced enough for the under third. When the teacher asked him about his parents he proudly related an almost romantic tale.

"My father," he said, " owned an estate in Kruszewnia by Schwersenz in the district of Posen. Later he removed to Pommern. Our family tree reaches far back. My forefathers were Pomeranian merchants who could trace their ancestry back to that passionate and criminal king of Sweden, Erich XIV, and his mistress, Agda Pehrsdotter. My mother was a von Tempelhoff, daughter of an old warrior family; her father was prominent in two campaigns, her great-grandfather was the General Georg Friedrich von Tempelhoff who was equally valued as a mathematician and as a militarist."

The youth was no discredit to his family. He soon became room senior (head boy). He showed no especial talent, only a thirst for knowledge. His first report contained a remark painful for him: he could not maintain his dignity. This temperament, the desire to command, remained with him.

Quickly he went from one class to the other. Years

passed by. He entered the head military school, became Second Lieutenant of Infantry, Regiment 57, and had to serve in the fortress at Wesel, a dreary and boring service. Thus his life began in drab monotony while his breast was still full of longing for action. Five years of this sameness. Then all at once he was commanded to Berlin to a military gymnasium. When this ended he was sent to the Second Marine Battalion in Wilhelmshaven. At the same time his Lieutenant's patent was dated a year earlier, a sign that his superiors valued him highly.

SECOND PICTURE

Usual military career. He was sent for a time to the War Academy, learned the Russian language, and after a three years' course made a trip through Russia with the concurrence of the General Staff. He became Battalion Commander, First Lieutenant, and Chief of the Division in the General Staff, then Colonel. From 1911 to 1913 he worked out the war plans for the German army. Shortly before war broke out he became Major at Düsseldorf, but almost immediately afterwards Brigadier General, then Major General at Strassburg. The doors to glory were standing wide open. In the prime of life, at fifty years of age, he climbed higher and higher until he reached the stars.

In Lüttich he obtained his first laurels. When the

ERICH LUDENDORFF

attack on the fortress and advance of the army threatened to go wrong he took over the brigade and found the way himself, after the pioneers had lost it. He pushed through with the brigade and took the fortress. The first lines were broken and the way to the city seemed open. Early on an August morning the troops would enter. Ludendorff drove on ahead in an auto with his Adjutant. He entered sooner than his troops and the surprised garrison surrendered to the two officers without resistance. The papers gave Emmich the credit for the capture of Lüttich, but it was really Ludendorff who had also worked out the plans for the attack. He carried out these plans with pluck and energy. The Kaiser was informed. Ludendorff was placed on the list of exceptions. It was he who told the monarch fourteen days later, when the Cossacks stood before the gates of Königsberg:

"There is only one who can help us and that is Hindenburg."

Ludendorff was commissioner to fetch the old general A. D. from Hanover and go with him to save the East. Blow after blow followed, the battles of Tannenberg, in Masuria, and on the Polish and Baltic fields.

Hindenburg and Ludendorff became the symbols of victory for Germany. But even then Ludendorff reached out for higher things. The military scale alone was not enough for him. The "hybris" crept into his heart, pride before which the old Greeks shuddered. Napoleon I arose again. Ludendorff reached out after political fame. The occupied eastern territory was now put under military rule. Reforms were introduced and the souls of the inhabitants drilled in barrack style. Remarkable that the Lithuanians, the Livonians and the Poles showed no understanding for the Kultur that was to be forced upon them for political reasons. Therefore, one must be more strict, more commanding. Yes, this was Ludendorff's eastern policy; simple and to the point. But he mistook these people for his recruits.

THIRD PICTURE

1916. The unfortunate attack on Verdun and the loss of the Somme led to Falkenhayn's fall — Falkenhayn, the salon General. Only after his departure was the bad condition of the army found out. Ludendorff finally went to the Kaiser and said: "If Falkenhayn is not deprived of the leadership, the army will be demoralized within a few months." Hindenburg had wanted to say it but could not bring himself to complain to the Kaiser. Ludendorff did it. The two now took charge of the whole army. Useless assaults and obstinate defenses merely for the sake of honor were abandoned. An elastic scheme of defense was now employed, Ludendorff's patent. The soldiers heaved a sigh of relief. What a senseless, even criminal waste of men had been going on. But that was not all. Ludendorff did away with bureaucracy in the trenches. Other generals replaced their own mental work by ordering reports, covering their mistakes with documents. Ludendorff saw that this was a waste of time for company and battery leaders. A new spirit had descended upon the earth.

FOURTH PICTURE

Ludendorff developed in great style from Quartermaster General to politician. Mr. Bethmann-Hollweg was gradually pushed to the wall. The political childishness which was to lead Germany to the brink of ruin began in Poland. Roumania then entered the war; the situation was critical. New armies must be conjured out of the earth. Poland must furnish one. As a reward she was to have national freedom, *i. e.*, what Ludendorff understood as such. The double proclamation of November 5, 1916, followed. Poland was made an independent kingdom — without a king! Come across with your soldiers now, was the command. Activists advised and implored them to leave the recruiting of a Polish army to them and the Polish Government. The Pole was skeptical. Ludendorff understood the psychology of the people better. He commanded, ordered the recruiting in Poland, invested German military stations with the necessary authority, and the result was — one hundred and eighty-one recruits for the new Polish army. Another version gives three hundred and nineteen as the result. Of course Bethmann-Hollweg got the blame — publicly at any rate. It was he who fought the U-boat war from week to week and month to month, because he feared America's entrance in the war.

But the marine bureau insisted and pulled the wires. Confidential circulars were published prophesying England's down-fall within a certain time if submarine warfare was introduced. The Alldeutschers, Conservatives and National Liberals began to shower Ludendorff and Hindenburg with thousands of greetings and resolutions against the slip-shod Government. Helfferich succumbed first to the U-boat hypnosia, then Ludendorff, who set the pace for everything, and the Chancellor had to submit. On the first of February, when the unrestricted warfare was announced, the following " Most High " command was issued to the navy:

" In the impending battles it is the duty of My navy to use the English method of starvation, by means of which your most vindictive and stubborn foe thinks to force Germany to her knees. It is your duty to use this method of warfare against the sea-trade of our enemies with every means at your command."

Ten months later they were more modest at chief Headquarters. At the beginning of December of the same year, Ludendorff said to a Viennese journalist: " We did not think our submarine warfare could starve England out in a few months." They only wished to increase her desire for peace. In many ways the supply of wood and coal was more important to England than food. Imagination! The forests of Scotland furnished wood enough, and as for coal, Cardiff alone produces the best coal in the world. Politically Ludendorff had exposed himself. And militarily? " The war shall not be given up as a draw," he said to the same questioner. " It will be decided favorably for us."

FIFTH PICTURE

Ludendorff's splendor grew and spread its rays in all directions. Not a few wished him at the head of affairs. The ever more visible dictator's claws pleased them. The deportations from Belgium aroused the whole world. These brutal measures proceeded from Ludendorff alone. He had not considered it necessary to confer with anyone about this fateful measure. Was he really a powerful man or did he only wish to appear as such before the world? The Chief Command began to deify itself. Only those newspapers were allowed to appear in which Hindenburg appeared as the Father and Ludendorff as the Holy Ghost. At bottom Ludendorff was but a small, political dilettante who had read himself big in the Alldeutscher *Posener Tageblatt* and *Pommerschen Tagespost*. One gradually began to see that his decisions in Home and Foreign politics were not made with that calm calculation and cool knowledge which characterized his military measures. One day documents will talk and the political historian will be speechless.

For his Home and Foreign ministry he had created a war press, and with this apparatus he squeezed every Government to the wall and the Reichstag along with them. Bethmann, Michaelis, Hertling, all strove in vain against this militarizing of politics. Ludendorff triumphed. He made an end of that ghost, "Russian peace without annexation," through General Hoffman.

SIXTH PICTURE

Hindenburg and Ludendorff reconstructed the army. They had taken it over from Falkenhayn in a not too healthy condition. Orders show how this was done: Sharper enforcement of compulsory obedience. Dessauer's system revived. Many officers silently disapproved. Everyone who has had anything to do with troops knows that little is accomplished by force. Troops and officers were too little bound by common interests.

The great offensive came to a standstill in the summer of 1918. At first it was only whispered about by a few at whom one shrugged one's shoulders. Most of the officers believed in the theory that pauses were necessary and that Ludendorff's hammer would strike a telling blow here and another one there, until the last great victory was pulled off in triumph. The Kaiser traveled to Aix-la-Chapelle and delivered his brilliant town-hall speech.

Ludendorff's hammer fell a few times more, once with success. And then all was over; Ludendorff told the party leaders in the Reichstag that he could only be responsible for the army for a few months at most. His nerves went back on him. The people's Government must save the Fatherland. In accordance with Ludendorff's world policy, German troops were scattered all over the world: in Finland, in Russia, in the Baltic provinces, in Lithuania, in Poland, in the Ukraine, in Crimea, in the Caucasus, in Mesopotamia, in Syria, in the Balkans, in Italy, in Austria,— and the west front got a blow below the belt, although the double front warfare was long since ended.

SEVENTH PICTURE

Ludendorff had proved himself incapable of judging the situation while there was yet time. Perhaps it was already too late after the first blow. Enemies of Germany would not have accepted an offer of peace even then, in which Germany did not recognize that she was beaten. If the militarists had given up then it would have prevented unnecessary bloodshed. But no—rather another try after too long a pause. When this instrument was dulled on the mangled bodies of men, when the third attempt failed, then Foch reached his goal. The command given to the troops at each of these offensives was to fight to the last ditch, utter ruthlessness with men and material. The moment these attacks became unnecessary the leader who ordered them was inhuman. The whole offensive was a huge mistake, as one could clearly see after the breakdown. There was a lack of knowledge of enemy strength. Ludendorff was wholly mistaken on this point. He lacked perception and penetration in regard to the reports made to him. The man who brought him these reports was the same who whipped up the German press for him: First Lieutenant Nicolai. Here is the tragedy of it all. On account of political incapability Ludendorff was blinded to military events by a tool who catered to his ambition. Even during the offensive Ludendorff could not see the ridiculousness of it.

"Foch still has forty divisions; thirty divisions; ten; now they are all demolished. Where is Foch?" so wrote a Berlin paper. Ludendorff looked on at this sort of reckoning and seemed to believe in it. He could not pass the test of greatness which knows the essential, discards everything else and rejects false honor. This inner victory, the victory over oneself, this ruthlessness which alone is great, seemed too bitter for this most ruthless of men.

The submarine warfare was the chief factor in the downfall. If Germany had not had faith in that, a cheaper peace might have been won. Ludendorff bears the responsibility for this step. It is an open secret that that there were very few boats. There was no foundation for other reports than the hope of new boats. Why did Ludendorff not investigate these conditions before giving the command? It can hardly be comprehended. Is it possible that he really was as superficial and credulous as they say?

Optimism held full sway in Rhineland industrial circles where he daily came and went. "A few weeks ago Hindenburg visited us. Everybody was on parade. It was like a visit from the Kaiser. Ludendorff looked unconcerned. He had a wave of the hand as much as to say: 'I'll manage everything.'" Such was the report of a Landsturm man.

Because Ludendorff had this motion of the hand no one on the whole general staff ever contradicted him. He suffered no contradiction. That really means that whoever contradicted probably lost his position. To comprehend the development of the whole misfortune one must add the ambitions and strivings of many other staff officers to Ludendorff's picture. Then one may delve deeper for the damage done to the German nation.

LEADERS OF YESTERDAY AND TO-DAY

EIGHTH PICTURE

Ludendorff drove his madness further after the collapse. The retreat succeeded but that was no fault of his. The troops once more stood firm as a stone wall. The enemy was thrown back. Ludendorff was again on top and ready to retract what he had yielded in a moment of weakness. Then came collision with the People's Government. He hoped to be able to make one more attempt. But it was already too late. A year or so ago he had been able to bring about Bethmann-Hollweg's fall by a simple " He or I." This time it didn't work. At the decisive moment Hindenburg dropped him for the Kaiser. That finished Ludendorff. He refused every order, every honor, every decoration, even the Imperial handwriting, as an insult. Hindenburg and Ludendorff left on two different trains, parted for the first time, the one to take up his work again, the other to retire on a pension.

The play is over. Go home, good people, go home. Ludendorff is no more. A nightmare has been lifted from your souls. A Napoleon has been sent to rest. He fled to Sweden when the revolution made an end of all those military spooks, and started without delay the work of writing his War Memoirs, a book of astounding volume considering its absolute emptiness as regards its contribution to military and political science as well as to the interests of civilization. Bourgeois and military reaction, after recovering from its shock over the downfall of its hero, is looking up to him once more as the coming savior of the Fatherland. And, by and by, Erich Ludendorff begins again to look upon himself in that light and to play, evidently to his own satisfaction, the part of the slumbering lion, growling in his sleep, ready to awake at any moment with the terrible roar of the king of the jungle.

IV

THEODOR WOLFF

Facts have always interested the average person, the general public, less than the personalities who stood behind them directing their course. Carlyle built up an historical theory on this fact. He reflected on the history of heroes. Antiquity idolized Plutarch whose biography everyone should read. Modern history has developed and been greatly influenced by an entirely new type of such " heroes," namely, the political writer. In democratic lands this pen heroism opened the way much earlier. France, or more correctly Paris, is the classical soil for it. In Germany the press was valued for decades rather as a cleanser of public morals than as a spiritual guidepost. At least this was the usual opinion in official or officious circles in regard to that necessary evil — the press. Under the pressure of war we also were converted and the papers could no longer complain of having to occupy a back seat. On the contrary, presumptions became so prevalent that it needed a firm character to resist the influence of all sorts of rumors. A good many German journalists failed to stand the test to which they were suddenly subjected. Most of them, in fact the compact majority, came to a compromise during the war. The people, who are not as simple as they look sometimes, scented this, and doubt crept into their despairing breasts.

Theodor Wolff belongs to those who maintained their backbone during all the various mental phases of the war. He was a fanatic for the truth, who even tried to fight against the daily lies of life. Wolff was originally purely literary; form was everything to him, aesthetics the main thing. Like all youths with their own mental life he composed poetry at school, but with all his youthful enthusiasm there remained a skeptical, a critical streak in him.

Critical Passages at Arms was the name of the first journal published by him during his school days. He was assisted by a number of school comrades, many of whom afterwards became pupils of Erich Schmidt. By encouraging a free stage he acknowledged his belief in naturalism, which was growing ever more powerful. Plays and romances soon arose from his pen. Kleist was not his model, rather Heine or perhaps Börne. But this is only a comparison, for he had a thoroughly independent nature whose strength was concealed by a mantle of gentleness and courtesy. His characters were spiritual, they were stamped with beautiful words and their lives were, unintentionally, a cult of beauty, an evening conversation with discreetly lowered lights.

A long residence at Paris was determined upon for Wolff. Here his talent for style and form received its last polish in the fascinating atmosphere of the Boulevards. He did not remain long at feuilleton work; politics soon captured him. At first it was the political heads of France, all the impulsive rhetoricians and political heroes that took his fancy. Then politics itself fascinated him, the eternal hither and thither, for and against of people, things and opinions; the eternal attempts to balance contradictions without ever coming to a harmonious whole: Thesis, Antithesis, and Synthesis. It was at the time of the political tension in France as well as in all Europe; the time of Dreyfus and Algeciras. Theodor Wolff was everywhere, writing and acting.

His literary reputation was already established when he returned to Berlin in 1907 to take Arthur Levysohn's place at the head of the *Berliner Tageblatt*. Many and varied were the things he brought home from Paris: a clean political shirt, a wide knowledge of people, a familiarity with the tricks of diplomacy, and an honest, democratic heart. He continually tried to induce Prussian Germany to lay aside the half-absolutism of the Friedrich period and to live up to the political standards of the rest of the Western Europe culture world. The new Theodor was keen and sharp and was not to be deterred by traditions. Inexhaustible were the weapons he used against the existing political system. He fought with wit and satire, with anger and indignation. At this time even liberalism had given way before the smooth business policy of Prince Bülow. In this black period, the *Berliner Tageblatt* fought almost single-handed against a policy which sought to veil and falsify the ineradicable differences between the Right and the Left. In spite of all opposition or more gracious wooing, Theodor Wolff remained firm. In most pronounced fashion he kept the Prussian franchise reform in the foreground. This was the apple of discord he continually rolled between the immoral marriage of the parties. The results after ten years proved him right. The Government itself finally proposed equal suffrage.

Theodor Wolff is undoubtedly one of the most attacked persons in the political life of Germany. Besides the integrity and strength of his character there is one thing no one can deny, and that is a political instinct of unusual certainty. The psychological is the fundamental trait that distinguishes his political writings. His Monday articles are the watchword for the political week. In the enemy's camp they tried to put an end to him by accusing him of journalism, of having little economical or social knowledge. But what is that? Is Count Hertling any the less a politician because he probably never belonged to a college of national economy? Or was Disraeli, Lord Beaconsfield, the novelist?

We are more interested in how Theodor Wolff contemplates politics and the State. We find the following definition in Schiller's letters to the Duke von Holstein-Augustenburg: "The State should not honor merely the objective and the generical in the character of the individual, it should also honor the subjective and the specific, and while spreading the invisible kingdom of morals and customs should not depopulate the kingdom of phenomena." It is the human that counts even in politics. This is not merely a platonic, democratic profession; it is a daily going out to do battle not only for ideas but for the people, that they may be brought a step further forward in the development of culture through the realization of the idea. This effort comprises everything — humanitarian thoughts, cosmopolitanism, democracy, ethics and aesthetism. Everything, and yet in this Wolff mixture there is something especial: the original personality behind all else.

According to Hegel, the State is a spiritual idea in the externality of human will and its freedom. That is what it should be at least. But a short time ago we were not so far as that in Prussia. The milestones on the way to it were: equal suffrage in Prussia, parliamentary system, international court of arbitration and universal disarmament. It is Theodor Wolff more than any other that deserves the reward for continually pointing to this necessity. Politicians were not able to withstand this suggestion forever. This struggle for equal suffrage, for a parliamentary system, and for pacificism, is faithfully reflected in his war-book, *Accomplished Facts,* a collection of Monday articles. Taken as a whole, it is a moral philosopher's balancing of accounts with the shadow side of war. " Like desecrated priest's garments," he writes in the introduction, " many have hung the worthless principles of justice, of truth and human dignity in the pawnshop. The joyless races of Philistines and Pharisees are increasing. Those who wish to keep out the enemy and guard the legacy of the noblest souls, feel themselves united for a common task. Out of this destruction it is they who will carry the true household gods into the future."

The revolution gave him a new impulse. The time seemed ripe for the discarding of the rusty, old, liberal party models, and so he became the instigator and actual founder of the " German Democratic Party " on a republican basis.

This is Theodor Wolff and his mode of life.

CHAPTER V

MATHIAS ERZBERGER

Through a narrow, creaking, little door we carefully enter the Dome. A murky twilight swallows us up. The last fine wisps of incense caress our senses. A tired little bell tinkles in our ears. Suddenly two forms arise, two men. Not hesitatingly like sinners or dreamers — they step out energetically like men who have a certain goal to reach. One is a priest, tall and thin, with an aesthetic face; fanaticism and indomitable energy gleam out from under gray lashes, energy that knows no compromise, no turning aside. A Jesuit father? The curious robe looks like it. His companion is rather short, round and well-fed. Red-cheeked, lively, bright eyes behind discreet, gold-rimmed glasses, blond hair, his face beams like the sun at noon-tide. Hans Thema has no chubbier, rounder, happier little angel on his flowery meadows than this.

Who are these remarkable figures? The priest I do not know, but he seems of high rank. But the other seems familiar; have I not seen him somewhere before? Is it not Mathias Erzberger? Yes, without a doubt that is who it is. But what is he doing here in this half-forgotten Dome, in this pilgrims' church near the frontier? Has a secret political mission sent him to this quiet corner? Is he holding a secret conference with a messenger from the Vatican? Not a soul here knows them. They can whisper and plot and throw out new peace nets undisturbed.

Absorbed in their conversation they pass by; in passing they hardly raise their eyes. A confessional reaches out its arms invitingly toward them. The priest pulls back the purple, shimmering curtain and seats himself. On the other side, separated only by a thin wooden wall with a barred grating, sits Mathias Erzberger. The confession begins with the words of St. Augustine: No one puts trust in himself in the impending discussion; in God alone do we put our trust. In God? Or in Christ's substitute, the Pope in the Vatican?

Who is this Mathias Erzberger that he undertakes to juggle with nations as with dogmatic formulæ and play the benevolent Providence? How does it happen that wherever we go we come across his tracks? In the press or wherever there is a political wound still festering he is the first to recognize the situation, to apply the knife to the abscess. Who is Mathias Erzberger whose spirit floats over the inky oceans of the *Germania,* that organ of Berlin's Center party; who not only writes for the party but also for the Government although he never signs his name?

Let him speak for himself:

"I was born in Buttenhausen on the 20th of September, 1875. You will not find Buttenhausen on the map, it is so small. It is situated in the quietest corner of Württemberg; cattle dealers are its excuse for existing. I was educated in Biberach, that ancient city with its medieval walls and its venerable church dating from the twelfth century. I wanted to become a teacher — a pedagogue — and had reached my goal at the age of nineteen. But my young blood left me no peace; it was not enough for me to teach the young idea how to shoot.

"At twenty-one I became editor and politician; after leaving the Catholic Teacher's Seminary I spent a few semesters at the Swiss Catholic High School at Freiburg, studying constitutional law and national economy. For seven years I was occupied journalistically for the Christian Guild movement. In 1897 I was sent to the International Labor Congress at Zürich; here at scarce twenty-two years of age I made my first tender attempts at establishing foreign connections.

"I had the power of persuasion and 'a gift of gab' so that I soon became the spoiled pet of the masses. It was no wonder that Biberach and Buttenhausen sent me to the Reichstag at the tender age of twenty-eight.

MATHIAS ERZBERGER

"Here I was looked upon as a Benjamin hardly to be taken seriously. But I had a head full of ideas and was soon the only one among the Center who really longed for deeds to free us from the sticky atmosphere of party politics. I peered like a thief in the night for opportunities. My thoughts wandered far, even across the equator to German Southwest Africa. The Colonies — here was my field! For only the specialist amounts to anything in the Reichstag. So it came about that on the 21st of January, 1905, I emerged from the darkness of specialization into the glare of the footlights and cockily disputed the claims of the settlers for damages resulting from the uprising. Those who go out to earn money must take the risk, I said. Such tones had not been heard from the Center of the House for a long time. They were accustomed to hearing such things from the Social Democrat side only. The gentlemen around the green table shivered slightly in this cool breeze and put their heads together.

"'What does this young badger want? What does he know about the suffering and distress in the Southwest? He is mixing in other people's business. It is impossible for the Center to identify itself with such things.'

"I admit it was not easy to convince the party of my opinions. But I pounded on the mass of material in my possession, which increased enormously in the course of the following months. The Colonial Government had not used its money scrupulously, so I wrote in the *Kölnische Volkszeitung*. Immediately the semi-official *Norddeutsche Allgemeine Zeitung* fell upon me with a lot of publications of documents trying to prove that my speech had been but empty talk. And I confess that my informers had not been absolutely reliable. But I was young and inexperienced.

"In 1906 I brought my whole party on the downgrade with colonial affairs. I had a scandal up my sleeve: the affair of Secretary Pöplau who had furnished me a great deal of material from Colonial Government records. Herr Spahn, our party leader, declared he was not convinced by Representative Erzberger; the latter had not proved any of his statements. Herr Spahn spoke in the name of the party, hoping to squelch me thereby. But the lightning ran down the rod and thunder did not scare me. Even the court did not bring me off my perch. In the Pöplau process I first maintained silence until Pöplau—under pressure—gave me permission to speak. But the court refused to put me under oath after hearing my statement. The others reproached me with this, saying the court wished to save me from perjury. My answer to this was that courts in general were not so squeamish, and moreover I did not know why they should make an exception in my case.

MATHIAS ERZBERGER

"In December, 1906, I exposed some German intrigues on the Spanish island, Fernando Po, that might have led to complications with Spain. I pressed the party to refuse credit for an increase of troops in the Southwest. I admit I was dismayed myself, when Prince Bülow arose solemnly from his place at the long Bundesrat table, took up a red portfolio, and in the name of the Kaiser adjourned the Reichstag. Naturally it was not easy for me in the party and I soon felt their displeasure. When the speeches of all the Center members were published mine was simply left out as if it had never existed.

"In a debate over Ostmark and Poland, Prince Salm brought up my name in connection with a theft in order to put me on the grill. I smile to think of it. The *Bayerische Kurier,* the leading South German Center paper, had published some especially intimate passages from the documents of the German Navy Verein. These documents were only to be obtained with the aid of a key from a private drawer in a writing table belonging to the Verein. They thought they had found the thief in the shape of one Oscar Janke, a messenger boy in the service of the Verein. He escaped and knocked at the door of a Jesuit monastery seeking admittance and perhaps absolution from his heresy (he was a Protestant at the time of the theft).

"The process continued and I made the following

statement before the prosecuting attorney: 'I refuse to give any information in regard to the following questions: whether it was known to me in what manner or through whom the article "Navy Verein Propaganda" appeared in the *Bayerische Kurier* of February 5, 1907, or whether the father or brothers of Janke had contributed any material or information for this article, because in answering either of these questions I make myself liable to prosecution. I beg to take an oath to this effect.' The proceedings had to be stopped. The prosecuting attorney frothed at the mouth, gathered up his books and papers, held his robe together which was flapping in the wind like a loose sail, and left the room. I had put him out of the ring and robbed him of his one day's glory. I didn't pass through the rigid school of church dialectics for nothing. If Theseus had attended a priests' seminary or even a Catholic high school, he would never have needed Ariadne's ball of yarn to escape from the Minotaur." He broke off.

The violet curtain was pushed aside; the priest arose from his carved Roman chair and stepped out, Erzberger by his side. In the meantime the church had gradually filled. The middle nave was already full. Feet trampled above in the choir loft. Youths and maidens intoned a pious cantus firmus. Under cover of the noises that now filled the church the two continued their conversation:

MATHIAS ERZBERGER

"I must have a short account of your doings during the war, my son," began the priest.

"Twenty-eight million marks," answered the other smiling, "I have given out for my mission. That proves my eagerness to bring about a peace in the sense of the church. The Government gave me everything I wanted of their own free will. I work in the Foreign Office with official stamps and ink-pads near my writing materials, and am often, much too often, sent on journeys. Herr von Bethmann-Hollweg makes use of me only too gladly. I took great pains in the effort to maintain Italy's and Roumania's neutrality; I have used considerable sums in Rome and Bucharest. It pains me to the bottom of my soul that Monseignor Gerlach was mixed up in that unfortunate treason affair. It must also be painful to the Holy Father, but the good cause — that of bringing the peace of Christ into the world — sustains me. I was in Stockholm, too, throwing out my lines toward Russia while the Little Father still trembled on his throne, and a Radziwill helped me.

"After that I was in Switzerland, most of the time with Ledochowski, Marchetti, Frühwirth, and Hoffman, who compromised himself as a member of the Swiss Bundesrat; everywhere you can find traces of me clinging to the Alpine rocks.

"It was I who said if Lloyd George or Balfour would

only listen to me for a few hours we could easily come to an understanding. It was also my project (I wrote it down somewhere in a confidential document) to invest German capital in English undertakings and English money in German banks, factories, etc. . . .

"And then I fought against the submarine warfare, too. I saw the political danger of such a step. And was I not right at least as far as U-boats are concerned?

" I haven't said anything about Austria yet or about Czernin, his letters, his desire for peace, or the peace resolutions I proposed and carried out. There was a row in the Center in July, 1917, when I brought up my project. His Excellency, Peter Spahn, trembled with indignation at my arbitrariness; in a fit of rage he accepted the post of minister in the Prussian Ministry of Justice, although this place was to have been adorned by his friend Persch. . . .

" I was in Holland, too, where I came into conflict with Thyssen, although he could have made such good use of me. I was complimented out of the executive council of the Thyssen concern because they felt obliged to be ashamed of me before the public.

" Have I not been a martyr for the cause of peace? Have I not prepared the way for the peace message of His Holiness, Benedict XV?

" But every crown, even the crown of service, has thorns and sharp ones at that.

"What have I gained by it all? Always driven to action, to deeds, my conscience would not let me rest while this frightful slaughter was going on."

"Right you are, my son. *Absolvo te. Ecclesia te coronat. Labora . . .*"

At this moment the choir began to sing with one accord the old song of peace which is the portion of all mankind — or should be his portion sometime or other.

From this peaceful island he returned to Berlin to take up his work once more. It was livelier than ever in his office on Budapester street. To his many other affairs was added the patronage over the Lithuanians, to whom he presented as king the Duke von Urach, his old Württemberg countryman.

Then he made preparations for a thorough change of system in Germany. Count Hertling must go, and with him the old régime. Prince Max von Baden appeared on the scene and in an hour of need grouped the People's Government about himself. The war cabinet was composed of State Secretaries, the Chancellor, and his substitute. Erzberger was not passed over; he became Secretary of State, Privy Councillor, and Excellence, Secretary of State for Propaganda, and after that head of the truce commission which brought Germany a not very joyful armistice.

LEADERS OF YESTERDAY AND TO-DAY

Ulysses' ten years of wandering were at an end. In his official Ithaca he at last found firm ground under his feet, and soon again cast about for new shores. When in June, 1919, the Democrats refused to sign the Peace Treaty and quit the Coalition Cabinet, and when in Weimar, five minutes before the expiration of the Entente ultimatum, everybody seemed to lose his head, Erzberger took a hand in the matter and the Treaty was signed. Erzberger became Minister of Finances and Vice-President of the Cabinet. He was confronted by new and weighty problems, such as the sanitation of the finances and the organization of a new and unified system of taxation, enough to cause any man to break down under the mental and physical strain of the task. Erzberger went at it with all his wonted energy that balks at nothing. A flood of new taxes poured over the German people. The budget of the Empire that before the war hovered around twenty-five billion marks, rose to ten times its former size, not counting in the (still unknown) indemnities and demands of the creditors of the Entente. The running expenses are growing continually. The value of the German mark on foreign exchange is continually sinking. But Erzberger's optimism is in no way affected.

" Erst mach dein' Sach',
Dann trink und lach'! "

he wrote, the smile of good humor and the glow of

robust health on his round face, into the guest-book of the Weimar "Fürstenkeller." Ten days after the bullets of a foolish youth whom the Nationalist fame of the murderer of Eisner, Count Arco, would not let sleep, had struck Germany's "strongest" man, he was facing his bitter antagonist and inveterate foe, Helfferich in the court room, ready to give and take, perhaps the only living German who will never know when he is beaten. The trial ended. As a result of the evidence in the court room it was announced that Erzberger had retired from public life. Was he beaten at last? And, if so, did he know it?

VI

GEORG LEDEBOUR

Georg Ledebour was an Emanuel Striese and had the speech and gestures of an actor. He was smooth-shaven, round-faced, not very tall, with frowning brows and piercing eyes. His rôle was Cato, the warning, threatening, morose, moralist probing the wounds of his own nation; a comedian, grown lame and toothless in his sixty-eighth year, still posing as the glorious Achilles when he was only fit for a Thersites.

Lebebourski was his nickname in the Reichstag, acquired at the time when no one protégéd the Poles as much as he. Ledebour-Bude leer (hall empty) was another pun because everyone ran, fled, scrambled out in any manner when he began his tirade against state and society. The period of his greatness was long past. In the days of Bülow he was still respected. He was then a Socialistic Thor flashing thunder and lightning from mouth and eyes. The Imperial Chancellor was in the habit of rising after one of his awful speeches to pour oil upon the excited waves. Ledebour beamed and the whole red Left beamed with him.

Before he became the heart of all things, before he

GEORG LEDEBOUR

became consequential and left off treading false paths, before he became the true leader of the people, before he arose to these spiritual heights, he was once but a man — a very small, human being. While he was attending high school in Hanover, his native city, he wanted to become an actor. Like Demosthenes, he, too, put pebbles in his mouth in order to strengthen his voice so that it might drown the mighty roar of the ocean (even if the only water in his neighborhood was the gently flowing Leine). Rolling speech and rolling eyes: the great tragedian was ready. But there's many a slip. The tragedian contracted some sort of trouble with his legs and had to give up a stage career. He became a teacher. At least he would have a patient audience of children. But it was difficult to climb to the stars on pedagogics. He was not a Comenius or a Pestalozzi; he sought larger audiences. He became author and editor, a democrat, a real beer Berliner democrat. Slouch hat, cape with fur collar, and knotted staff were acquired, and a pince-nez with a long, silken string showed the new tendency. His motto was: For folk and freedom.

At first he wrote for the *Democratische Blätter,* and then for the *Berliner Volkszeitung* until 1889–90, just as Bismarck, the terrible Ivan of home politics, gave his last official snort.

Ledebour took to the platform with whole Berlin-

Pankow at his feet. He talked to the crowd with hands and feet as well as mouth. Bismarck and the Junkers he flayed alive; he charged the Socialists with fixed bayonet. Socialistic ideas? Nonsense. Slavery, prison house. The only real freedom was democracy — I repeat it once more, democracy!

Twice he was to discover freedom elsewhere. Ledebourski later gnawed his way through to social democracy and here discovered the only real, genuine democratic ideals. *Vorwärts* offered him a seat on the editorial staff. (These times are long past — *Vorwärts* and Ledebour are now as fire and water.) Here the savage raged and rampaged worse than ever against serfdom, and dogma (but only in the church, not in the party), against capitalism, and at least three times a day he brought out a hurrah for the social battle. He raged in ink and screamed with the glue-pot, and daily cut in a thousand tiny scraps the whole Junker brood, capitalism and tyranny of the church. August Bebel prophesied the whole jamboree for the near future; Ledebour pounded the whole putrified, Philistine society into a mess, took the consequences of his actions, left the church — this Union of Souls — and became a dissenter. From this hour on he frequented smoke impregnated atmospheres preaching against priesthood and brain-muddlers, with wildly waving arms and ten outspread fingers.

GEORG LEDEBOUR

Although his eyes rolled in beautiful madness, he was not exactly loved by his party. Bebel couldn't stand him. Ledebour was always at the front on every party day, always a desperado, always the most radical, not to be beaten even by Adolph Hoffman, always thoroughly opposition, never ready for any sort of understanding or compromise. Bebel avoided him; said behind his back that he was not politically respectable. Many other party members gave him a wide berth, too. In Dresden at the great party house-cleaning, Bebel gave him a good going-over, a thorough, blasting, blighting dressing down. But Ledebourski went on speaking with even more sweeping gestures. In the meantime he was sent to the Reichstag from Berlin's sixth voting district, one of the most populous sections of the city, where Wilhelm Leibknecht formerly reigned supreme. Thenceforth he represented the Rosenthaler Tor and Pankow districts with the dignity of Robespierre's moral guardian.

Have you ever heard him speak in the Reichstag? There he is enveloped in the cloak of conviction; every word that springs from his round, little mouth is a pearl. His right arm is stretched out, hurling insult after injury. He moves his eyes around recklessly, the pince-nez loses its hold, the marrow of your bones begins to freeze. The judge of the world has arisen, the great reckoning is about to be made. Just at this moment the president tinkles his little bell. Once — twice — thrice! Ledebour goes on. A call to order falls upon his head. He hestitates. After a few minutes another warning. The present order of the world won't give up without a fight. Once when statistics were taken it was discovered that Ledebour had ignored fifty calls to order in one day.

He was witty, too,— witty, sharp, and cutting as a razor blade. He prepares his speeches himself at home days ahead. At the proper moment during the sitting a party comrade interrupts. Swift as the dot on an "i" he gets a little well-prepared satire hurled at his unsuspecting head. If it didn't strike home, which happened sometimes, Ledebour would repeat the comedy until the gallery applauded.

He was one of the first to play split party politics. He it was who discovered the "Independent" social democratic freedom. Always ready to help, he traveled now here, now there, cheering up the masses. His specialty is foreign politics, especially Eastern. He long maintained a warm friendship for Russian revolutionists. This is comprehensible for they only loved one another from afar.

The 9th of November arrived. Ledebour's highest ideals were fulfilled. The theater demagogue mixed in "big politics." They placed him at the head of the executive committee of the Workmen and Soldiers' councils. He took infinite pains to set the whole nation against Berlin. His ambition knew no bounds. Everybody else was to lie down, the Government along with them. He even came into conflict with his bosom friends, Haase and Dittmann, in the cabinet. In short, the whole affair pleased him no longer; he thirsted for more blood, so he went over to Liebknecht, Rosa Luxemburg, and Eichhorn, to the Sparticists and communists, to upset the Government and put himself in its place. Already he dreamed of Imperial Dictator, Ledebour, Georg I.

But the second revolution failed miserably in spite of the many sacrifices, and one night Ledebour was called from his bed and arrested. He was placed on trial, was acquitted, and,— for the time being,— Ledebour retired to country life in order to regain his health.

VII

ERNST VON HEYDEBRAND UND DER LAASE

Conspicuously short in stature, a dark brown, sunburned face, an uncared-for, pointed, grayish beard and a thick mat of hair like a close trimmed hedge on his head, from the middle of which a lock ventures forth, Mephistopheles-like, on his brow; a shiny, iridescent, holiday coat (military fabrication), frayed trousers; such is Herr von Heydebrand, insignificant little man, as he goes through the streets. No one would suspect the "uncrowned King of Prussia" in him; rather, an old clothes peddler.

But he is a born ruler, an East Elbian Junker of the purest water, landowner, master of Gellkewe, Klein-Wiesenthal, and Klein-Tschunkawe. Here on these lower Silesian estates with the Chinese-Hottentot sounding names he rules supreme — here is his voting district for Landtag and Reichstag. He is no longer young, having already passed his sixty-seventh milestone. In Jena, he got his degree of Doctor of Law, passed the usual state examination, and became assistant judge in more than one court. He then entered the Government of Opplen, became Landrat in Keselin, 1882, and five years later Landrat in

ERNST VON HEYDEBRAND UND DER LAASE

Militsch-Trachenberg. After eight years he left the service and devoted himself exclusively to politics. He has been a member of the Prussian Diet since 1888.

Herr von Heydebrand was not spectacular. For many years no one heard anything from him. He was only one of many, but he grew with the people and the material, because he was industrious and did not regard his seat as a sport. As one by one the front men died off, he took his place in the conservative faction. A few years before the war he became leader of the Reichstag faction after Herr von Normann departed this life.

There we must leave him. He was always on the spot. When all fled before some speaker from the Left, he remained. As party chief he maintained strict discipline. He was not only general but also little corporal of the party. The members of his faction might remain away from the sittings, they might listen to the speeches over a glass of wine in the Parliament restaurant, they might even go walking, but they *must* be present when the ballot was taken. That he insisted upon and the members parried like recruits. At the second reading of the Prussian franchise bill, when the Left too hastily counted on the absence of a large part of the Right, they were all in place to a man. Herr von Heydebrand had commanded " Right about face," and the Government suffered its first heavy defeat.

LEADERS OF YESTERDAY AND TO-DAY

Five men made the politics in the House of Representatives — Heydebrand, Zedlitz, Persch, Friedberg, and Pachnicke — all ripe in years and wisdom, cool and objective. The most temperamental was Heydebrand; he ran like a Daimler motor with continuous little explosions. For hours he could sit with folded arms listening to speeches from the Right. All at once he would spring up and run like a weasel to the speaker's platform. He would not stand behind the desk — that would have hidden him from view — but stood between the desk and the Government's table and began to fire away.

His talk sounded like the rattling of a machine gun. He did not speak like most of the others, wearily reading from a manuscript; a tiny visiting card on which were jotted a few hurried notes was crumpled in his hand. Rapid and witty was his talk; interruptions did not disturb him. He received them, worked them over in a trice, and answered with pointed phrases that sometimes dripped poison. He would also suddenly pause, turn each word in his fingers like a gem, and then snap the glittering, venomous things at the Government or the Left. One listened to him willingly for he is a personality with his own charm. But after all he is only a desperado, a fencer seeking a weak place for his slender steel, more dialectic and tactical than clever, far-seeing policy.

ERNST VON HEYDEBRAND UND DER LAASE

Heydebrand fought many a battle against the landowners, against the agrarian demagogues, but they were stronger than he. As the cleverer, he gave in, and after that he stood by them through thick and thin. In the battles for finance reform in 1909 he tormented the party to the utmost, broke the Conservative-Liberal block, drove the whole Government into a corner, made them renounce what they had repeatedly determined upon, undermined their authority, and forced Prince Bülow to retire. And why? Because he fought tooth and nail against the inheritance tax — a tax which must come sometime or other as he said himself. In the same way he damned the three-class-system franchise which he had once declared " almost ideal." But the result was that both the inheritance tax and the franchise system came about in the natural course of events.

In regard to foreign politics the Conservatives were already in Alldeutscher (Pan-German) waters before the war broke out. Bethmann-Hollweg steered for reconciliation; Heydebrand stoked the fire against England. Then came the famous clash between the two. While the Conservative party leader spoke against England, the Crown Prince sat in the Court loge listening to his words. I can still see him sitting there, both hands resting on his saber propped up in front of him. And while Herr von Heydebrand, downstairs in the noisy hall, was casting his fire rockets across the channel, the German hereditary prince applauded enthusiastically by lifting one hand and letting it fall repeatedly on the back of the other.

It was a stream of boiling water which Bethmann let loose in the face of his opponent. Heydebrand tried to preserve his dignity, but his face visibly changed color. He had not expected such a cannonade from the State Hemorrhoidarius. After that he left the field to Count Westarp and devoted himself almost exclusively to the Landtag. One saw him rarely in the Reichstag, but he never failed to appear when Bethmann spoke. Then the little man was wont to growl and mumble from his place almost directly beneath the Chancellor. From this moment on Bethmann-Hollweg forfeited his position with the Conservatives.

A battle unheard of in Prussian history began against him. Everything Bethmann did was used against him in one way or another. There was no regard for foreign countries, for the Monarch, or for the one attacked. He was accused of shilly-shallying because for a long time he could not approve of introducing submarine warfare. When he warned of the danger of America's entering the war he was laughed down. Herr von Heydebrand, who very seldom took to the pen, published an article in the *Kreuzzeitung* whose twenty lines swept aside the danger. "America and Us" was the title of this composition signed with his full name.

ERNST VON HEYDEBRAND UND DER LAASE

Again Herr von Heydebrand rode the wrong horse. Bethmann's attempt to approach the Social Democrats and Free organizations was one of the worst reproaches against him. Insinuations were poured into His Majesty's ears. The idea of a League of Nations supported by Bethmann-Hollweg was mocked and laughed at, and finally Herr von Bethmann-Hollweg was overthrown. Heydebrand remained victor upon a field of corpses. But it was a dearly bought victory, for Bethmann's legacy still remained: the wish for peace, compromise, parliamentary system, and election reform. A solid majority was formed in the Reichstag consisting of the Center, the Progressives, and the Social Democrats; the Conservative party was left in splendid isolation. They were merely passed over after this. They made all the more noise in the House of Representatives, where they held sway for a little while longer.

But Herr von Heydebrand was played out with one full sweep when Germany's military position grew so bad and all signs pointed to a storm. "This is the end of the Conservative party," he moaned. "We have been betrayed."

From this hour even the Conservatives were for equal suffrage and after the revolution Herr von Heydebrand retired from political life, a "compromised personage."

VIII

ALFRED VON TIRPITZ

I must devote a few critical lines to the man who more than any other German politician has tried to influence public opinion through literary channels. Journalism in the widest sense of the word. I begin pedantically with the first chapter.

His propagandistic activity dates back to the year 1884. Even then as a young staff officer, he composed a memorial for the Reischstag, advocating the construction of one hundred and fifty torpedo boats. After this little episode his name was forgotten. Wholly unknown to the public, he continued his service in the marine department. Twelve years later he again emerged from oblivion with another memorial. In the meantime he had become Rear Admiral. This time he went directly to the Kaiser and laid an extensive, costly plan for a new fleet before him. When the fact became known and parliamentary circles began to get uneasy, the Government published the following article on the 12th of September, 1896:

"Plans for increasing the navy have not been laid before His Majesty nor before any other responsible

ALFRED VON TIRPITZ

person. Rear Admiral Tirpitz has never been called upon for any such plans nor has he ever been in a position to be called upon for such. It is not the intention of the marine executives to deviate from former customs of sending in a statement of their needs to the Reichstag, nor will they ask the Admiralty for any extensive plans or propositions for the navy."

A few months later, in March, 1897, the Imperial Chancellor, Prince Hohenlohe, as well as Secretary of the marine department, Herr Hollmann, insisted that the new propositions be placed in the budget. Herr Hollmann especially insisted in regard to the Tirpitz document: "Neither the allied Governments nor the Reichstag can bind themselves to any such formal regulations for years ahead. It is quite impossible, even if both desired to do so, for the simple reason that the art of naval warfare is quite as changeable as that on land. It is quite impossible for the marine department to say what may be needed ten years from now; if conditions change then you may be sure our requirements will change with them."

But Tirpitz, who was not yet knighted for his great services, pulled the strings from behind, and when the Reichstag Budget Commission did not swallow all the naval demands, Herr Hollmann got his walking papers. At the same time Herr Tirpitz, who until now had been commander of the cruiser division, was called to the head of the marine department. Here was a pretty kettle of fish! His memorial, which the Reichstag had just denied, was now authoritative. A new bill must be introduced covering expenses for such plans. This bill excited almost universal opposition. Even the Free Conservative and Liberal press were against it. The *Post* wrote sarcastically that the navy would be rendering a very poor service with such airy plans and that altogether it was bad policy. Tirpitz listened but was not convinced. He knew the value of the press, therefore a press bureau was organized for the marine department. Under the harmless title of *Reports,* the papers were furnished free of charge with news from the naval department. The official papers were wholly exploited for this purpose, and gradually the other papers bit. After years of such press work, Count Hertling declared it unbearable and Representative Müller-Meiningen requested the Chancellor to take care that the possibility of a double foreign policy did not arise on account of the marine department's special press bureau. The Reichstag did not scent the danger at that time. The Kaiser sent comparative statistics to the Reichstag and even put himself in the service of the marine as general enlightener: " The trident belongs to us! " and at another time, " National power means sea power; one cannot exist without the other." When Prince Heinrich was sent to strengthen the di-

ALFRED VON TIRPITZ

vision in East Asia, in a toast to his brother in the castle at Kiel, the Monarch remarked: "If any one undertakes to hinder us in the acquirement of our rights we will go for them with the mailed fist!" And Prince Heinrich answered: "Fame does not entice me, nor laurel wreaths; one thing alone moves me and that is the desire to preach the Gospel of Your Majesty's holy person to all foreign lands who wish to hear it and to those who do not."

On the 30th of November the Reichstag finally accepted the new navy bill: nineteen battleships, twelve large and twenty-four smaller cruisers. The fleet was increased one third, the construction and payment — almost a milliard — was to cover a period of six years. This program was accepted by a majority; at least they would now have a rest for six years. But Tirpitz left them no peace. The press propaganda of the marine bureau was not enough for him. The advertising drum must be beat a little harder. On the 30th of April the German Navy Verein was founded and began its course of enlightenment in great style. Correspondence was sent out, lectures given, placards and statistics placed in every railroad station, and thousands of bureaus, even the "movies" were drawn into the service. The suggestion began to work. One year and a half later Tirpitz came out with a new navy law, again made in the dark. It was all arranged with the "Most High" before he went to Baden-Baden to obtain the approval of the Chancellor.

The new program meant doubling the program of 1897–98 for the years 1901 to 1917. Once again Tirpitz had walked over the rights of the Reichstag. Liberal speakers pointed out the danger of alarming the world with such a program, but it made no difference, Tirpitz carried off the victory. Would one at least have peace until 1917? Not a bit of it. In less than twelve months another breach of trust leaked out in the shape of a secret mandate of the marine Secretary dating from January 6, 1902. It contained still another navy law modestly expressed for 1904–05. A pretty little maneuver was discovered in it: instructions to the officials of the marine department to stuff the payroll for the Reichstag. Later he tried to justify this, but the Reichstag had grown distrustful. On the 7th of February, 1902, Eugen Richter said:

"I have seen many ministers come and go, but I have never seen any who were so little to be trusted as Herr von Tirpitz. I cannot but say that Herr von Tirpitz's decree contains a confession of dissimulation and a lack of honesty unfortunately not met with for the first time."

Richter was not called to order by the president. Even Dr. Oertel, chief of the *Deutsche Tages Zeitung*, writes: "Does Herr von Tirpitz really think he has

ALFRED VON TIRPITZ

any claim to the confidence of the Reichstag after this?" Herr von Tirpitz pocketed everything with a smile. He still had the confidence of the monarch. He heard these bitter truths more than once. Said Representative Leonhart:

"We see once more the pupillary security of Herr von Tirpitz's explanation confirmed."

The strictly Conservative president, Count Schwerin-Löwitz, was called upon for order, but he smilingly shook his head with the remark that he was not in a position to call to order for the reproach was meant for the Imperial marine department. With light sarcasm Dr. Struve said more than once that the State Secretary's flights into higher mathematics were difficult to follow.

Three times more, although everything was supposed to be settled until 1917, the State Secretary came before the Reichstag with new bills for 1906, 1908, and 1912. New cruisers, new battle ships, the old song.

It was old Bismarck who said with prophetic insight: "I am very mistrustful of parade ships which serve only as a mark of prestige; when things become serious they are no good. The most important thing for us is a strong army. That was also Moltke's opinion. I am thoroughly convinced that we shall have to fight our decisive battles on land, even those in regard to our colonial possessions. Therefore no fantastic plans that we shall have to fight over later." And further: "I should like to know what assailant is thought of. I hope not one who may first become our foe when un-German greed for prestige and a hurried equipment at sea serve to drive him into a coalition against us." Tirpitz was of another opinion. He built and built and drove England into that coalition feared by Bismarck.

Although he was really the father of the war, he pretended not to know it. Perhaps he really did not know it, which makes it all the more incomprehensible for a politician.

In November, 1914, he was interviewed by von Wiegan, an American journalist. He said: "I was one of those who would not believe this war would come." In the spring of 1914 his speeches were so cheerful and self-confident that Herr Bassermann cried out with joy: "I am convinced that the relaxation between us and England is made possible only by our large navy. This relaxation is the best proof of the correctness of our naval policy."

Oh, yes, the gentlemen representatives all gradually learned to dance to his music. He knew how to arrange everything so beautifully. Now they were invited to visit the Imperial yards at Kiel and Danzig, now to inspect the ships or attend a maneuver, and always the Secretary of the Navy was the most gracious host who had drilled his people on board to be equally obliging. He always managed to talk confidentially to one or another of the parliamentarians. He assured liberal men that he was thoroughly liberal in his views — of course he must preserve a certain reserve for the public — approached the Center with a friendly mien, expressed his sympathy for the Catholics, promised to see to it that strict church discipline was maintained on board, and what was no joke — he transplanted several Catholics to that purely Protestant island, Heligoland, in order to impress the Center. He soft-soaped them all. Even when the war unraveled the whole submarine question, he knew how to maintain the aura of a dignified statesman falsely accused. With that we come to the second chapter.

We have already said that von Tirpitz's naval policy was the real cause of the World War. Have we had any success at sea from his plans? Here we see the tragedy of the policy for which Tirpitz had most of the German people hypnotized. We had to dismantle a part of our ships because the material was needed for submarines. Our warfare at sea was almost entirely confined to U-boats. Tirpitz not only did not encourage the building of submarines, but actually hindered it, because he did not understand the significance of this weapon. This was his second great political mistake. While England and France feverishly built submarines, Tirpitz would hear nothing of them. He adopted the "watchful waiting" policy. Technical people and progressive politicians pressed him; he showed them the cold shoulder and went on building large ships even after the war started. One could not put commanders, captains, and admirals at the head of a U-boat, and there must be some place for such high personages. There were put in service before the war: in 1906, one submarine; in 1907, one; in 1908, one; in 1909, two; in 1910, one; 1911, five; 1912, five; 1913, six; and in 1914, up to the outbreak of war, four.

In November, 1914, Tirpitz boasted to von Wiegand, the American, that he could cut England off with big submarines; he could torpedo every ship that left the harbors of Scotland or England, and starve them out. The whole world pricked up its ears. What real power had the Secretary behind him then? Fantastic numbers were mentioned. In February, 1915, he came out with the proclamation: War against merchant ships! Eighteen submarines with oil motors — old iron from 1909 — and perhaps a dozen newer ones with Diesel motors were at his disposal according to Representative Struve. This was the iron curtain he was to drop all round England! Then came his demand for unrestricted submarine warfare. Bethmann-Hollweg prophesied war with America in this event. Tirpitz laughed at him. In January of 1918 he said to the Berlin correspondent, Paul Lothringer, of the *Neuen Poster Jour-*

ALFRED VON TIRPITZ

nal: "America's help is, and always will be, a myth." He was overthrown in 1916 on account of his desire for unrestricted submarine warfare. Now he brought everything he could catch in his nets against the Government. A campaign without equal was begun against Bethmann-Hollweg, and Tirpitz was boosted in the *Alldeutsch,* the Conservative, and the Liberal press, as a "misjudged genius." In a memorial he assured the public that England could be starved out in six months. In 1916 he had already told Representative Erzberger that it could be done in six weeks. After January, 1917, we had the submarine warfare and, as a result, war with America and several other seafaring nations — and England began to triumph.

But Tirpitz knew how to avoid criticism for several months. It is not difficult to guess how. He could occupy Conservative publicity mongers who lauded him as the prophet of the U-boat war and damned Bethmann-Hollweg, while the other side was compelled to keep silent because the censor demanded it. Tirpitz became the powder keg of home politics. Civil peace was shattered on account of him and the battle about his person.

So we come to the third and last chapter.

The German Fatherland's party was founded. Tirpitz at the head associated with the wildest annexationists. It was chiefly directed against England. In the most diverse assemblies he began his song of hate for England which invariably ended with the words: "We must have the coast of Flanders!" One must not forget that Tirpitz had not always had the words "perfidious Albion" in his mouth. He once said: "I grew up in friendship for England and the English; as seaman I have never failed to recognize the great side of this world power." His offshoot, who wore father's blue coat with fewer stripes on the sleeve, fell into British hands at the very beginning of the war in 1914. Later when the joyful telegram was sent from London that son was well and enjoying himself at tennis with the wife of the Naval Minister, Churchill, the English papers wrote: "Surely 'Gott strafe England' is not a prayer that Herr von Tirpitz be received into the lap of the family. His wife and two daughters were educated in Chattenham College; his son, now our prisoner, is an Oxford man. Tirpitz himself has never concealed his admiration for the English character; he has introduced the methods of our soldiery at home down to the last uniform button." And to-day? Well, times do change; but no quicker than Herr von Tirpitz.

He puffed the Fatherland party with money and advertising; sent his agitators up and down the land. Advertisements were let off by the thousands, like the sparks from skyrockets. They penetrated bureaus and officers; placards in glaring colors were pasted everywhere: in stations, on houses, on the streets, and the *dernier cri* in political propaganda — a storm of telegrams — was rained upon the Kaiser, the Crown Prince, and Hindenburg. With huge sums at his disposal Tirpitz organized a campaign against the Government and the Reichstag majority. His confidants reckoned he would be at the head of things by February, 1918, at the very latest. Then Count Hertling would be laid on the shelf. And the coast of Flanders? Gradually the leading lights explained that they would leave Belgium intact. The Belgian question was a moral factor for the whole world. Without a moral victory the world markets would remain closed to Germany after peace was declared, and Germany's economical life would receive a mortal wound. But Tirpitz overlooked all this. Like a naughty child he would have his Flanders coast. Of course, for strategic reasons, " we must have a naval base against England."

These " practical politics " collapsed in a few months, and this same Fatherland party saw itself compelled to support Prince Max's cabinet and mix with the democrats if they did not wish to lose the ground beneath their feet. During his twenty years of political activity Tirpitz always rode the wrong horse. He can look back over an unbroken chain of mistakes and failures. Even the Alldeutscher papers, whose idol he was, reproached him ten years ago with " not having made the most of his opportunities."

LEADERS OF YESTERDAY AND TO-DAY

When the Tirpitz navy started the revolution, Tirpitz made tracks for Switzerland in order to write in Switzerland's rarified mountain air his memoirs — a fairy tale, though not devoid of strong personal interest, filled with acrimonious charges against his colleagues and former associates, but still — a Tirpitz book. Perhaps he is Admiral of the Swiss navy now.

IX

FRIEDRICH NAUMANN

There is a large cleft between the secular Evangelical Church and ordinary mankind. Secularized Christianity has so many thousand interests that have nothing to do with love or charity. Consistories and synods have shoved the whole bureaucratic apparatus of the church somewhere between heart and intellect, thereby winning the purely worldly protection of the throne and the selfish, economical interests of all those who surround the throne. Those who look upon Christ as a Comforter, as a Redeemer, those who are weary and heavy-laden, were pushed aside and left to wander their own way in socialism.

This Royal Prussian Evangelical Secular Christianity stripped itself of the last vestige of human charity during the war; over the horsehair garment of forgiveness they drew on the mailed shirt of battle. With my own ears I have heard from the pulpit a justification of hate. The father of literary Satanism would have rejoiced at it. It was good tone in church circles to belong to the Fatherland party whose motto was war *ad infinitum.* Traub was an example of this.

LEADERS OF YESTERDAY AND TO-DAY

This discordance between the teachings of Christianity and the ways of life has always appalled the genuine preachers of God's Word — especially the modern technical world, the world of machinery that atomizes human work and renders the life of the masses joyless. Shall I name a few of these genuine souls such as Kierkegaard, Emerson, Kalthoff, Jatho? There are many more.

Friedrich Naumann's name must not be omitted in this list of upright men. He, too, sees the misery of the masses with clairvoyant insight that penetrates to the innermost recesses of the soul; would like to help but can do so very little as an individual. As pastor, as theologian, shall he only talk and talk? Shall he seek to satisfy mankind with the hard bread of ancient history, with comparisons from a book of the past? Or shall he spring into the horrors of daily life, leave the word for the deed? He chose the latter.

Naumann was born in 1860, in a little Saxon village, Störmthal; entered the Nikolai gymnasium at Leipzig and was then sent to the Fürsten school at Meissen. He studied theology at Leipzig and Erlangen, but mere preaching did not satisfy him. Like a friar of the Middle Ages, he entered the Rauhe House at Hamburg. His field was home missions. He came to Glauchau, that dingy, poverty-stricken factory district in Saxony, where there were only chimneys and chimneys; where the people walked with crooked backs through narrow, smoky streets. He was then called to Frankfurt am Main as pastor of the southwest German conference.

It was the year 1890 that Bismarck's era came to an end. In the world of literature young Germany appeared with her crass naturalism. The youthful Kaiser proclaimed the beginning of a new social epoch. In an intoxication of enthusiasm the intellectuals turned to socialism. The Bismarckian nightmare seemed lifted from humanity. Naumann took his place in the ranks of those who were pressing forward, believing he could do good work from the pulpit. His first book appeared: *The Social Program of the Evangelical Church.* "What is Christian Socialism?" he asks in a second book. In 1894 he wrote his *Social Letters to Rich People,* at the same time working on other ideas: *Jesus as a Man of the People, God's Help,* etc.

He had the courage of his convictions. A number of fellow-thinkers gathered to his support, theologians, students, people who longed to break loose from the heartbreaking monotony of an officially approved and stamped career. The National Socialist party was founded; national socialism and democracy on the one side, army and navy enthusiasm on the other. Eugen Richter made fun of this socialistic imperialism, but it made no difference to them. The *Hilfe* became the organ of these disciples with Naumann as publisher,

LEADERS OF YESTERDAY AND TO-DAY

Martin Wenck, a theologian, as editor-in-chief, and Friedrich Weinhausen, also a man of God, as general secretary of the new party. Everything looked rosy. In Berlin a paper called *Zeit* was started with Naumann as editor. Paul Rohrbach lent his services, but it did not last long. After three quarters of a year the paper went to sleep, appearing for a short time thereafter as a weekly.

In the meantime, these young theologians plunged into the election battle. In 1898 Naumann was candidate in Jena-Neustadt. Bassermann carried off the victory. Five years later he again ran for the Reichstag but in vain. Only two National Socialists reached the goal: Hellmut von Gerlach and Heinz Potthof. After this unsatisfactory showing the party regarded the affair as hopeless and was soon after dissolved. Some went over to the Social Democrats and the others, among whom was Friedrich Naumann, went over to the Liberal organization. Naumann had devoted himself in the meantime to political journalism. Every year two or three books appeared from his pen.

The confession of his faith is laid down in *Democracy and Imperialism*. He held both factors as compatible. In the *Norddeutschen Wirtschaftspolitik* he justifies the economical demands of capitalism but leaves the question open, whether in the future, when the whole world is capitalized, socialism will not come of itself. Aesthetic problems interested him, pedagogy also; he cast a network of new thoughts over everything, wrote on the most diverse subjects. His publications were enormous.

At the end of 1907 he finally reached the Reichstag. His hour had come at last, so it seemed. Now he could get busy in great style, and the nation, the world of culture, would listen to his words. His first speech on the relationship of employers and employees in the modern industrial world created a sensation in the press. It was far above petty party quarrels. He uttered great thoughts in splendid language. Only those in the party thoughtfully shook their heads, and slowly a glass wall was built around him. The "slave uprising" began. He might talk all he pleased on party days, he could let himself be applauded by enthusiastic audiences elsewhere, but in the Reichstag he was frozen out. Here reigned *minores dii — arteriosclerosis —* and new blood was not desired.

Naumann, who had discovered the fairy flower of liberalism, was himself pushed to the wall. This was shameful but unfortunately true. He was not practical enough. That may be; a trace of romanticism was not to be denied. Intuitively he found interpretations, formulas easily comprehended by the masses, for even the most rigid political conceptions. He had a tendency to formulize his policies. His happily discovered word, "Middle Europe," in a book of the same name, led to the suspicion that Germany intended prolonging the present economical war indefinitely.

He speaks as he writes, picturesquely, clearly, often playing with allegories. His voice is not full, not even sympathetic; it is rather creaking, almost hoarse, but a wealth of ideas and viewpoints adorns all he says.

He failed at the last Reichstag election in Heilbronn in 1912. He was finally elected by Waldeck-Pyrmont where anti-Semitism courageously lifted up its head. An inner demon drove him over onto new shores. He continued his Samaritan service every week in the columns of the *Hilfe*. He found new ways and aims for the Home Mission — Home Mission as he saw it. In the National Assembly he found a field for his political romanticism. He became the leader of the Democratic Party. But just when his hand reaches out for new plans, the heart of the great exponent of eternal human rights stops beating and — Naumann is no more.

X

WILHELM II

A fresh, lively youth, bubbling over with spirits, Hinzpeter once complained that Prince Wilhelm was a wide-awake and gifted lad but difficult to lead. In a letter of another teacher, we find the following: "You reproach me for not being more strict with the Prince. You do not know the difficulties with which I have to contend. Wilhelm has slipped out of my hands altogether and is wholly in the hands of the military camarilla; the unfavorable influence of the Potsdam guards shows itself more plainly from day to day." Wilhelm was sent to the Potsdam Government to acquaint himself with the work under President Achenbach. Mad, hobbledehoy days began.

The Prince played the silliest pranks with the beautiful Kitty at Kietz's, and in the casino of the First Regiment of the Guard he was the wildest of all. Champagne glasses were smashed on the candelabra; mirrors served as targets, and drinking was carried on on a wager. The Potsdam Philistine shook his head disapprovingly, but in a residence city it was the custom of the subject to speak only when he was told to by the authorities.

Marriage did not put a stop to this fermenting process. Grandfather grew old and older (would he live forever?), father was ill with no hope of recovery, and Wilhelm began to play with the idea of very soon ascending the Imperial German throne.

Flatterers crowded around him, people looking forward to future favors. He made plan after plan in secret: "When I am Kaiser the world will sit up and take notice; I shall make Germany great and set the pace for everything: politics, music, art, literature — in short, Kultur. If I could only get rid of that nasty old bear, Bismarck, respectably!"

The hour came that placed him at the head of Germany's destiny. He was now a man of thirty, but juvenility remained in his blood, as shown by his plans, his continual self-aggrandizement, troubling about his own soul, this eternal grasping after new impressions, lack of perseverance, craze for publicity, and monstrous egoism.

The men who surrounded him were more cunning than he; Generals began to kiss his hand, he liked to see it in his Caesar romancing. Bismarck, the brakeman and admonisher, was thrown out and now began the race for royal favor. It fairly rained orders, titles, and patents of nobility. In the Golden Book of Munich, this monarch ever greedy for homage, wrote: *Regis voluntas suprema lex.* And the people, lowered by these words from mastery to mere subjection, hurrahed and threw flowers at him in their enthusiasm. He journeyed from city to city making speech after speech amidst waving flags and garlands.

A characteristic picture: On the 1st of July, 1901, the Kaiser was on board the little cruiser, *Nymphe,* in the bay of Lübeck, in order to watch the torpedo practice for Kiel week. There was a large following on board. In the intervals between shooting, the Kaiser would enter the chart room in order to attend to the signing of documents. Tirpitz laid the papers before him and the Kaiser scrawled his enormous Wilhelm underneath. When this grew monotonous he glanced up at an officer standing near and said: "Terrible, this Tirpitz with his ink! I would rather have a glass of champagne." "At your service, sir," rumbled the officer, and ordered a bottle of Heidsieck. (French champagne had to be labeled "Burgeff-Grün" because the Kaiser wished to believe he had good old German wine before him.) The Kaiser drank all but a little, then went, glass in hand, on the bridge and called down to the deck where the whole gathering stood in gala uniform: "Ha — Hahnke, you like champagne, too!" and threw the rest of the glass onto the people below. "Too gracious, Your Majesty," stammered the gentleman underneath, bowing deeply. The Kaiser, in high, good humor, again entered the chart room and demanded something to eat. He was handed caviar on toast. He smeared the butter and caviar from one piece with his forefinger, licked his finger off and went back to the bridge: " Ha — Hahnke, you'd like some bread, too! " and threw the piece of toast down upon Hahnke and his consorts. Another " Gracious, Your Majesty," was the devoted answer. Then in a whisper His Majesty asked an officer standing near about the speed of the boat. " Ha — Hahnke, how many knots does this ship make an hour? " As the Colonel stammered his lack of knowledge: " Ha — Hahnke doesn't know anything. It makes twenty-one knots an hour and with you it's twenty-two."

The conceit of the Kaiser was partly due to the people around him; he valued them as they wished to be valued. He treated them like old clothes. His lackeys suffered under his moods and temper and his use of men in the ministry, in the army and in society, was ruthless.

Another picture: It was on the 6th of September, 1901, before the slender, Gothic, Rathaus tower in Danzig. The Empress' bodyguards were sent to Langfuhr to join the Emperor's Hussars. The entrance into the city through the triple-arched Grüne Tor on Langen Markt was particularly impressive. The parade stopped before the Rathaus at the entrance to Langgasse, with Mackensen, the new commander, at the head, the Kaiser

WILHELM II

opposite, both on horseback. Dr. Clemens Delbrück, mayor of the city, bade him welcome. A thousand people thronged the streets, windows and balconies, waiting to join in the "Hoch" which was to be led by the dignified Behren, president of the city council. All at once a whisper went through the throng. An adjutant rode up to the Kaiser; he inclined his head and the adjutant whispered something in his ear. The monarch's cheerful face suddenly grew black; his horse reared. William McKinley, his friend, the great president of the United States, had just been shot by the anarchist, Czolgosz, while visiting the exposition at Buffalo. The relentless Goddess of Fate lifted a warning finger in the midst of this jubilation. "Remember," she whispered to the Kaiser, "remember America."

He tried to put his stamp on the whole human culture of his period, from pointed mustache to poetry, music, art, even machinery and architecture. He went mad over monuments. Not even the tiniest village dared be without a Kaiser Wilhelm monument. He grasped the lyre and composed that frightful song to Aegir; he interfered with the work of the stage manager, painted pictures, and corrected architectural designs. Everything he touched must be pompous, senselessly overloaded with adornment. This Wilhelm tam-

tam baroque was little suited to the simple, industrious German people who, more than any other nation in the world, worked day and night, unceasingly, to bring their nation up to the standard and win the respect of the world. This parvenu succeeded in gradually infecting the whole people with his blow-your-own-horn propaganda. When the architect brought the plans for the Kaiser Wilhelm Memorial church, Wilhelm rejoiced at the star above the cross on the steeple, praising it as an original idea. The architect did not venture to tell him the star merely pointed to a remark in the footnotes. This was the Kaiser — superficial, incidental, casual.

Only one thing he recognized in foggy mysticism as being above him, and that was God. Lucky for God that he remained invisible and let Wilhelm talk on without putting himself in the painful position of having to contradict him. On the Seventh Sunday after Trinity, A. D. 1900, at the time of the troubles in China, the Kaiser preached on board the *Hohenzollern,* taking as his text Exodus xvii, verse 11: And it came to pass, when Moses held up his hand, that Israel prevailed: and when he let down his hand, Amalek prevailed. "Our text for to-day brings a profound picture before our souls. Israel wanders through the desert from the Red Sea to Mount Sinai. Suddenly the heathen Amalekites cross their path. A battle ensues. Joshua leads Israel into battle; sword rattles against sword; a bloody struggle begins in the valley of Raphidim. While the armies rage to and fro the pious men of God, Aaron and Hur, climb to the top of the mountain and lift up their hands in prayer. Below in the valley, battling troops, above, the praying men; that is the battle cry of our text. Who does not understand the meaning of this image? Again the Amalekite hordes have arisen in the far East. With fire and sword, with power and cunning, will we pave the way for European trade and European culture; Christian customs and Christian faith shall win the victory," and so on. Fourteen years later Wilhelm prayed and prayed all through the war, but his enemies carried off the victory. He was always playing theater; like a bad comedian he mistook fantastic imagination for reality and seriously believed himself to be the prophet of his people, the Chosen One of God. The men surrounding him strengthened this notion although they themselves saw through this clerical spook. Bismarck said he was a man who wanted to celebrate his birthday every day.

"Just leave social democracy to me," he remarked to one of his ministers as, undisturbed by the Old Man of the Sachsenwald, he sowed a few political wild oats.

Indeed, at first Wilhelm was full of grand ideas, social reforms, etc. He wished to satisfy everybody — Social-Democrats, Liberals, and Center. This wise, thirty-year-old father of his country wished to display his imperial graciousness to all. The social reform proclamation of February, 1890, was issued; duties on grain were reduced; Bismarck's laws against social democracy, the Center, and the Poles, were rescinded; a great school reform was announced; in public speeches the monarch promised his people the beginning of a glorious epoch. This lasted scarcely three years. Even on the 20th of February, 1891, he complained that he was neglected and shook his fist at the bogey man in Friedrichsruh. "He spreads the spirit of disobedience throughout the land; veiled in seduction he attempts to confuse the will of my people and those about me. He uses oceans of ink and printer's black to fog the ways that ought to be clear to everyone who recognizes my principles. I will not be confused by him." And then came the reaction.

The rudder was twisted toward the right. A zigzag policy was carried on after the "foolish people," "the parties who followed only their own interests," refused to recognize the Kaiser and opposed the Junkers. Step by step the prison bill was introduced, the return to Ostmark politics was made, to high tariff, to banishment of Social Democrats, and the Prussian three-class

WILHELM II

suffrage system was strengthened. Old Prince Hohenlohe spilled soup on his frock coat in joyful embarrassment as the Kaiser raised his glass to drink to the health of the new Chancellor. Bülow knew how to curry favor with his Imperial Lord with all sorts of witty ideas and mishmash politics. Bethmann-Hollweg was the only one who wanted to carry on an honest policy, but he could not get rid of his conservative, bureaucratic past, was always in terror of his own courage, and thought to accomplish something by continual compromises.

When the Kaiser finally decided to democratize Germany it was too late. As a conservative politician, Count Hertling declared he could not participate in such an action; he asked for his release, explaining to the Kaiser that he could not accept a parliamentary régime without denying his Lord, by the Grace of God. But the Kaiser had already learned something; he knew even in those gloomy September days that the war was lost and that he must make his peace with the people. So he became hard of hearing and remained.

When he ascended the throne of his fathers there were eleven Socialists in the Reichstag; in 1912 there were already one hundred and twenty. When he lost his crown there seemed to be nothing but Socialists. All the other dynasties lost their right of existence and with them the Bundesrat and the Reichstag; the whole kingdom threatened to disunite.

LEADERS OF YESTERDAY AND TO-DAY

In thirty glorious years he had governed the German nation to pieces.

His foreign policy was still more deplorable. Even here he wanted to do everything himself, wanted to be his own Minister and Chancellor. He was an extremely bad psychologist. He thought he could make everything all right by friendly personal relations with neighboring potentates. He drove into Bismarck's clever, diplomatic net with clumsy but admirable lack of perception, tore down the wires leading to Russia to throw himself into the arms of decayed, old Austria-Hungary. He provoked England with his loud-mouthed naval policy, and Russia at the same time, with his sudden love for the sick man on the Bosporus. He came out like a glorious Lohengrin against France's Morocco policy and threw down the gauntlet before Casa Blanca. Always the same game: ambition for personal greatness and Germany's world importance, which embittered the others until they decided to stop the mouth of this bragging parvenu by a diplomatic coalition.

This nightmare which had caused Bismarck so many sleepless nights, although it was then but the product of fancy, now became reality, and war broke out.

"I did not wish it!" Certainly not. Wilhelm was much too weak a character to wish for it. But he had acted as if he wanted it, and even if he did hope for peace to the last moment he let himself be influenced by his generals who were stronger than he. For fear of being considered a coward he let himself be pressed into a war that could have been prevented (he clung to the great example of his ancestor, Frederick the Great), committed a breach of neutrality against Belgium, and gambled on submarine warfare with the others. At the beginning of his career he could not get out of Bismarck's gigantic shadow; now the shadows of Hindenburg and Ludendorff oppressed him. Now that the time for action had come, when he could really be the great leader of his people and the nation, he was only a very small, helpless, dangling, little man, a comedian whose make-up melted in the glaring light of day. He occupied the whole four years between whimpering prayers and imperialistic revenge speeches or posing before court painters, now as a Roman Imperator, now in the field-gray uniform of a general. And the result? Millions of dead and wounded, a lost war, bankruptcy of a nation, degeneration of a whole people, loss of territory, and inner revolution. Men, mothers and children lift up their hands against him. This is the glorious epoch he promised his people.

After a heavy night the gray morning of the 9th of November dawns. The Kaiser arises to leave the train in which he has spent the last night. Hindenburg awaits him in the Villa Fraineuse. Staff officers appear as delegates to report on the condition of the troops. The universal opinion is: " Against the enemy, steadfast; against his own comrades no one will fight. The field troops are retreating in disorder. The Rhine bridges should be guarded. All communications with home are cut off. Telephones are mostly under the control of the Soldiers' Councils."

Crushing! In the meantime the telephone rings continually from Berlin: the Kaiser must abdicate. The monarch does not respond. Has His Majesty not yet decided? No. Finally the Imperial Chancellor proclaims the abdication himself in the hope that the *fait accompli* will ward off the revolution. Too late. At last the monarch declares himself ready to lay aside the Emperor's crown but not that of Prussia.

But Hindenburg, Greener, and Hintze insist, and a quarter of an hour later Admiral Scheer leaves the royal apartments with a very red face. He enters the front room and reports to Adjutant Count Dohna-Schlodien, commander of the *Möve:* " You no longer have a Commander-in-Chief."

Event piles upon event. The Kaiser must leave Spa as quickly as possible. He does not wish to and cries out in despair: " I have always known before what I should do, but now I do not know how to help myself."

WILHELM II

One of the adjutants, on being asked for his opinion, replied: "If I were to decide for my own person, I would remain. If the troops will not fight for Your Majesty we will form a body guard of officers. We can occupy almost every point for this purpose."

At ten o'clock Herr von Hintze warned His Majesty again: "Your Majesty, it may soon be too late."

Hastily the last measures were taken, everything was packed, and at five o'clock in the morning the court train pulled out in the direction of Le Reid, the next station on the Spa-Pepinster line. The Kaiser followed in an automobile headed for the Dutch frontier station Eyst.

No flags, garlands, or maids of honor accompanied the last journey; no hurrahs or music. He fled like a thief in the night. In Amerongen he enjoys the haven of refuge Holland has granted him, listening with bitterness in his heart to the voices of the outside world that penetrate into his asylum, refusing to believe that the days of "Gottesgnadentum" are gone and clinging to the hope of a return to power, and of imperial splendor, as of yore. He is convinced that the German people have paid him with shameful ingratitude.

XI

CLEMENS DELBRÜCK

Clemens Delbrück made a stately appearance. He is large with a slight inclination towards embonpoint, has a short, drooping, light-blond mustache, almost bald head, lively, light blue eyes, with a firm, steadfast expression — a splendid, imposing personage in the gala uniform of a State Secretary, but at bottom only an official type of the war period. For many years he was persona grata with the Kaiser without being conservative. He trod the narrow path between conservatism and liberalism, turning now to the right, now to the left, with obliging readiness just as the moment demanded. Always he had one or more compromises ready to hand and always a ready solution for resistance or disinclination on the part of the Ministry, Bundesrat, or Reichstag. This clever, adroit politician who, as soon as the war broke out, began to flirt with democracy, has now been out of office more than two years. In 1916, when the food system threatened to go to pieces, he was one of the first of Bethmann-Hollweg's stand-bys to leave. The grateful monarch hung the Order of the Black Eagle around his neck

CLEMENS DELBRÜCK

and knighted him for his services. He went because as an advocate of free trade he could not approve of a socialistic food system. He retired from office ill, tired, and resigned; built himself a quiet little Sans Souci in Jena, and settled down as professor of political science at the old Thuringian university where Melanchthon, Schiller, Fichte, and Hegel once taught. He wrote a little book with suggestions for reforming higher Government careers. Then, after two and a half years he again entered public life. As von Berg's successor, he took over the presidency of the civil cabinet for a few weeks only. With the downfall of the Kaiser he was finished.

A Delbrück had once before occupied a prominent place in Prussia. Although he had been the Chancellor's right hand, he, too, had to give way to political changes and new ideas. In spite of undeniable service, he, too, was the victim of a transitory period after the war of 1870. In spite of his clever diplomacy, Rudolph Delbrück was a strong character who continued to fight Bismarck's high tariff system even after his retirement from office.

Clemens Delbrück, former Secretary of State and Vice-Chancellor, was not less gifted as a Government official. What he lacked was association with the fluctuating life of the people, their thousandfold emotions, hopes, and desires; he lacked the ability to form quick resolutions, to take things into his own hands, or to form original ideas. For a few years only did he rise above the narrowness of Prussian officialdom, and these were not enough to enable him to gain a wide perspective or to enter broad paths disregardful of the many considerations within a bureaucratic system. He was soon a "maid of all work" because he could accommodate himself quickly and soon became acquainted with his material. But in the course of his varied career he could not separate himself altogether from the green table.

At twenty-nine years of age he was Landrat in Tuchel. In this isolated West Prussian spot he came into close touch with landed property owners and seven years later was called to Danzig as councillor of the Agricultural Department. His chief, Gustav von Gossler, former Minister of Education, soon recognized his superior talents and valued him so highly that he recommended him as Baumbach's successor as Mayor of Danzig. This conservative man took his place at the head of the Government of a city renowned for its liberalism, a city which had been represented in the Reichstag for decades by a Heinrich Richter.

He stood the test. Important days came for Danzig. The Kaiser's interest was awakened for the old Hansa city on the Vistula. He sent the Posen Hussars to join the Danzig bodyguards. Before the slender, dig-

CLEMENS DELBRÜCK

nified, old town hall tower, Delbrück greeted the Kaiser and General Mackensen, former aide-de-camp, now at the head of the Hussars. The monarch was pleased with the Mayor of Danzig and his impressive speech; even in 1901 it was known that Delbrück was the coming man for Wilhelm II. Scarcely a year passed before he was at the head of the West Prussian administration. Prince Bülow had just started his Ostmark policy — Delbrück seemed the right man for the helm. He was given three tasks; besides an extensive colonization scheme, he was to look after the educational and economic development of West Prussia.

The funds for the colonization commission were raised in 1902 from two hundred to three hundred and fifty million marks; besides this, another one hundred million was thrown out for the establishment of domains, a concession to the landed proprietors. This systematic colonization scheme soon became a two-edged sword causing the price of land to increase enormously. As an offensive policy it was unsuccessful, for the Poles soon refused to sell any land to the Germans until Bülow used the weapon of expropriation against them, also without much success.

The thought of industrially and commercially lifting the East to a higher plane also met with little success because economical reasons for such a policy were lacking. One could not shut off the Ostmark from

Poland and Galicia with high tariffs and then expect to found industrial centers in this dead corner of Germany. The lack of raw stuffs and coal made competition with the West impossible and the Eastern market was as good as closed.

The educational scheme also followed a somewhat unusual course. The Ostmark appropriations were meant to bind teachers and officials to the soil, but because this was not always complied with it made much bad blood. The only accomplishment worthy of note was the foundation of a technical high school in Danzig and the little educational work done in the provinces.

Without any reproach to himself, Delbrück was unable to make much of a show with the Ostmark policy after three years of activity. In 1905 he was called to the presidency of the Prussian Board of Trade. This was the third time within a comparatively short period that he had occupied a responsible position. But here, too, his powers were not developed to the full. There were big beginnings but small results. In 1907 he laid down a proposition which was to remove all difficulties in the way of opening up mines; in November of the same year he drew up measures which were to influence the high prices of coal in favor of the consumer. But everyone knew that he had promised more than he could fulfill, like "Long Möller," his predecessor. Once again, at the wish of His Majesty, he interfered for the benefit of the masses against the coal barons. After the terrible misfortune at Radbod in November, 1908, he introduced a bill for the institution of a Labor Controller. In his speech he declared: "It is a battle for the soul of the individual." The ever-increasing danger of anarchy and terrorism seemed of more importance to him than danger to the lives of miners which was the main object of the bill. It only meant a means to gain his purpose — the policy of the green table.

But even here he had to satisfy himself with a compromise. In June and July, 1909, he threw himself in the breach for Bülow's policy and fought against coal export duties and mill taxes. Although the majority listened to his speech with insulting indifference on that hot summer day in the Reichstag (with the exception of Bethmann-Hollweg), he was one of the most energetic tax-diplomatists of the crumbling Government.

He got his reward. Bülow resigned. Bethmann-Hollweg was his successor, and Delbrück, as Secretary of the Interior, became one of the corner stones of the new Government. Two powerful laws were passed under his leadership: a summary of the whole insurance regulations with a clause pertaining to the care of widows and orphans, and the employees' insurance law. But on the whole, his social and economic policies suffered under halfway measures and compromises.

LEADERS OF YESTERDAY AND TO-DAY

One thing must be admitted in his favor, the Department of the Interior grew to enormous proportions under his leadership. In time it was to become a reservoir for the most heterogeneous collection. Even Count Posadowsky groaned over it, and the idea of dividing it into several departments was more than once considered. The war added a thousand other tasks to the already overburdened department. Even the intricate food problem was loaded onto this office which soon became an automatic law-making machine. This must have been too much even for a man of Delbrück's type. Added to this was the helplessness of the whole affair. It could make laws but had neither control nor executive power.

After a while he saw that things could not go on in this manner much longer and suggested that the food department be separated from the Department of the Interior. This was done, and he retired. Dr. Helfferich was his successor. Clemens Delbrück had seen the dawning of a new political order of things, but was no longer permitted to participate in the work of reconstruction.

He was a man with a passion for detail, who often overlooked the big idea, who did not allow himself to be governed by creative principles. All in all, he loved his office. This was his strength and his weakness at the same time.

XII

HERMANN PACHNICKE

Octavio, Baron von Zedlitz, dethroned chief of the Free Conservative party, and Hermann Pachnicke, chairman of the Progressive Landtag faction, had much in common. Both had acquired an unusual routine during a long parliamentary and journalistic career. For a time scarcely a week went by that they did not publish their political opinions in the red *Tag*. Both had grown gray over it. On the coat of arms of both stands the word "Prudence." They glide over the polished floor of politics in felt slippers in order not to scratch its surface.

Twilight was their sphere; their stars gleamed only in the night. For both are tacticians, political schemers; usually they stepped upon the speaker's platform only when there was something to debate. One of their special themes was the franchise problem. They forged a thousand compromises behind the scenes, Dr. Pachnicke more than Baron von Zedlitz.

They were somewhat different in temperament, although both were political foxes, but Herr von Zedlitz could at times speak out plainly. This was the liberal streak running through his conservatism. Herr Pachnicke was only a rationalist. Each word must first pass the gates of reason before it ventured across his lips. In general, he wrote as he spoke, in well-ordered sentences with not a single error of construction. It was just the same in his private conversation. In the Reichstag they say he kissed every word he spoke and tried to win everybody by rolling his forget-me-not eyes graciously hither and thither. He was a man after Bethmann-Hollweg's own heart, who hesitatingly uttered his friendly feeling for democracy before the public and under four eyes made all sorts of promises without thinking much about the time of their fulfillment. The other two eyes were not seldom those of Herr Pachnicke, who knew how to keep himself fresh in one's memory. Forget-me-not!

Dr. Pachnicke was born in Spandau and is already past sixty as his dignified white beard shows. He was a journalist, having studied philosophy and political science in Berlin, Munich and Halle. He began his literary career with a study of the philosophy of Epicurus. He has ever been true to a carefully regulated enjoyment of life. One should not strive for every pleasure that offers itself, so Epicurus teaches. One must first ascertain where there is a maximum of pleasure or a minimum of pain. Sufficiency is the true wisdom of life; in order to preserve health and the ability for enjoyment one must avoid sumptuous and expensive pleasures. Pachnicke's interest in the social problem may be traced to this. With Berlepsch he wrote a book on the necessity of a national labor bureau. He was never a doctrinaire. He worked for the interests of the Government when Caprivi brought up the military reform bill. After the two-year service for the infantry was conceded and after a heavy conflict with Eugen Richter, who was not in the habit of giving way even an inch, he went over to the elements who broke away from the People's party. He was sent to the Landtag every year from Königsberg and represented the district of Parchim in the Reichstag. When Count Hertling entered office his name was mentioned among others for the cabinet. But the discussion came to nothing.

In holiday time Pachnicke always left Berlin and retired to his home in Hopferau, which belonged to the Bavarian district of Füssen, close to the borders of Tyrol, where tower the snowy Alps. After a short rest he would again descend from his mountain heights into the flat lands of parliamentary activity — just the opposite of Henrik Ibsen's *Brand*. Brand came near ending as priest of the ice church; his cruel bluntness, his " everything or nothing " drove him into a fearful loneliness. When Pachnicke descended from his mountains, he always found connections; he contemplated accomplishing *something,* not everything. Goethe's censorious words were not meant for him: "What, you make the world? It is already made!"

And so as a politician he worked on the basis of things as they were.

XIII

OTTO HAMMANN

The war was a great opportunity for the journalists. Every office, every war society had its literary bureau with some journalist at the head of it. It was different in the old days. Bismarck had a "piece of white paper" reserved for him in the *Norddeutsche Allgemeine Zeitung,* and for quite official things there was the ponderous apparatus of the *Reichs-und Königlich Preussische Staatsanzeiger*. Besides that, he was on confidential terms with a few reputable journalists but that was all. It is possible that a few newspaper correspondents were nourished by the Guelph Funds, those "Reptile Funds," in order to smuggle official things into the Independent press. Otherwise the Government troubled itself little about the press, did not consider it qualified for respectable society, and officially it was mentioned as a mere object.

When Bismarck left the Chancellor's palace in 1890 it was not much better. True, the man of Sachsenwald was an independent coworker on the *Hamburger Nachrichten,* kept a few journalistic bodyguards and made it as difficult as possible for the new course of events. But the people in Wilhelmstrasse kept on treading the old path; in 1894 the German Government had but one office for the press for home as well as foreign political questions, and this office was occupied by one chief and two clerks whose principal duties consisted in making clippings from home and foreign papers. There was not even a telephone. Rudolf Lindau worked with only one assessor or vice-consul and there was time enough for him to read the proof-sheets of his master's new novel. The chief occupation of the press bureau consisted in sending Prince Bismarck a review of the day's news and carrying out the directions that came back from Friedrichsruh in regard to these reports. These directions were often written in such a way that they needed only a head and a tail to make them ready for publication in the *Norddeutsche Allgemeine Zeitung* or elsewhere.

Caprivi, the Chancellor-General, like his predecessor, contented himself with one confidential journalist, Dr. Otto Hammann, Berlin correspondent of the *Münchener Allgemeine Zeitung,* the *Schlesische Zeitung,* the *Hamburger Korrespondenten,* and the *Pester Lloyd.* His political beliefs were rather hazy, a sort of National Liberal-Free Conservative mixture.

Hammann was born in the little Weimar town of Blankenhain. He studied law and passed his examinations, but two years later he went over to journalism.

When he first met Caprivi he had been an independent writer for fourteen years in Berlin.

"On a June day in the year 1892, I received an invitation to come to Wilhelmstrasse 77, for a consultation with the General who had taken Bismarck's place two years before. A few articles in the *Pester Lloyd* which had attracted the attention of the general were responsible for this honor. He accompanied me to the Chancellery garden. On the corner of the middle path stood an old chestnut tree under whose branches we took our seats at a table standing there. That was the first time I had even seen him closely."

Caprivi started the conversation by remarking that this beautiful park was the only pleasant thing about his position. Then he spoke of his predecessor:

"It is impossible to attack him as I would like most to do. Being an old soldier, he would beat me at it. What is his reason for his vehement actions against the new regiment? He cannot, and will not, take over the office of Chancellor again. There is only one explanation left and that is passionate bitterness with the wish to humiliate the Kaiser. Hate is the mainspring of the greatest deeds. It began in the Eschenheimergasse."

So Hammann relates in his memorials under the title of *The New Course*. He was in a painful situation; he was a Bismarck disciple, and yet, through his personal contact with the old General he began to have a strong liking for Caprivi. His writings are not exactly voluminous nor do they show deep penetration of people or things. They are smooth and pleasing, light and flowing, as if written for *Garden Leaves* (a magazine for women), and even the most simple is not likely to stumble upon a problem that will cause him any brain work. This reporter has written descriptively, uncritically, touching upon trifles more than important facts, contenting himself with the mere periphery of the thing. But perhaps herein lies the value of the book. It is not documental secrets that speak, but the human, all too human, side that runs through it. Sometimes he quotes from Schiller, Bismarck, and, if I am not mistaken, also from Goethe.

A friendly intercourse developed from this first meeting with Caprivi. Hammann placed himself journalistically at the disposal of the new course of events. "In the middle of December, 1892, during the battle over military reform, the two-year service period, the Chancellor told me he expected a dissolution of the Reichstag. Therefore it was necessary to spread as much information in the election districts as possible."

Now, for the first time, a systematic press campaign was begun, reminding one almost of Bethmann-Hollweg's press-assault. "On the upper floor of the right wing of the Chancellery Major Keim set up his quarters and began a fruitful propaganda activity with the utmost confidence in its success. Everything that could, or would, help in any way was put in action." Baron von der Goltz-Paseka, General von Boguslawski, General von Kamecke, and among the scholars, Gneist, Conrad, and Wagner, to work for the new leader, who later used this same method of suggestion for the benefit of the Navy Verein and the Military Verein.

In 1894, at Caprivi's wish, Hammann became an official in the political department of the Foreign Office. Baron von Marschall was then head of the department, but the secret regent was really Herr von Holstein, "the man with the spots on his inner iris, who maintained all sorts of subterranean connections" and who rode us into the Morocco adventure. In spite of all the mistrust and political prejudices against him he was a man of upright principles whose style combined logic with the finest and clearest diction. His articles were sharp and cutting; even Hammann could not do as well. And that was why Holstein did not wish to find a competitor in Hammann; grumbling and bearish he put the cabinet question and was then appointed director of the political department. Thus Hammann's press department came under his jurisdiction. Holstein said afterwards that Hammann had rebelled and after his departure it was he (Hammann) who instigated the press mutiny against him. "It was not that at all," said Hammann, "and there was not the least bit of posthumous revenge about it. The whole Holstein crisis, which lasted from the time of King Edward VII's visit in June, 1904, to April, 1906, was sometimes like a Shakespearean comedy."

Hammann broke off his chronicles just at the point where they might have become more interesting, in defense of Caprivi: the acquisition of Heligoland, the trade agreements, military reform, and resistance of the anti-socialistic laws. This was during the time of Herr von Hohenlohe's chancellorship, but he did not enter into Bülow's or Bethmann-Hollweg's policies although he had had an opportunity to observe the work of these men more closely perhaps than that of the others. It may be that he was silent for reasons of discretion, in order not to say anything detrimental or even personal about those who are still living.

But, you will ask, has this man who mocked the inadequacy of the official press apparatus had any influence for the better upon it? Not in the least. He started an underground press organization and out of the large number of Berlin journalists, he chose a few to whom he retailed news. He smuggled a few official things into their papers for the sake of their good will. In time he became more and more unapproachable. The leaders of those big papers who valued their independence naturally cut him and sought their information elsewhere. When the war broke out one recognized all of a sudden how much irreparable damage had been done by the depreciation of the power of the press. The curtain was suddenly drawn back from in front of a rubbish heap.

When the foolishness of the former situation was recognized and a new relation was sought between the government and the press, some believed, because it was war and Germany was in a state of siege, that the press should be commandeered like the army. The most ridiculous censor regulations were held over the newspapers' heads like a knout with iron barbs. Gradually, during the course of the war, it became a little better. A really confidential relationship arose — and Herr Hammann left the office with the titles of acting Privy Councillor and Excellence, to devote himself to journalism once more. That is, he became neither correspondent nor editor, but a member of the executive committee of the *Transoceanic Nachrichtengesellschaft,* whose aim was to establish a news bureau independent of Reuter.

Once only did I have an opportunity to speak with him in his official capacity. This was in a snug corner of the German Society's clubhouse. It was after an unexpected suppression of the newspapers. He promised to act as intermediary although I knew he, himself, was responsible for the suppression.

XIV

ADOLPH HOFFMANN

It is a very busy day in the Prussian House, a great day. The diplomat's and minister's loges are filled with curious onlookers; even the tribune is full. A garland of ladies lends animation to the scene. Beneath in the assembly room representatives are buzzing like bees. Little groups form here and there; everywhere lively discussions and gesticulations are heard. One minister after another dribbles in: Breitenbach, Hergt, Schmidt, Spahn. Orderlies run about with papers and documents. Herr Drews, Minister of the Interior, comes and with him Dr. Friedberg, vice-president of the Ministry. The gentlemen by the portals of the Government room step aside respectfully; Count Hertling, president of the cabinet, enters. Immediately Count Schwerin-Löwitz, chairman of the House, swings the bell a few times and announces the opening of the session in his weak, irritable voice. Election reform stands on the calendar of the day.

The battle of intellect begins. The debate waxes hot. Often there are tense, dramatic moments. Everybody fights like a lioness protecting her young; the Right,

ADOLPH HOFFMANN

the Left, the Center, the Government. The onlookers do not conceal their feelings. Hisses and applause, cries of approval or disapproval fill the intervals. The representatives are crowding around the speaker's platform in order not to lose a word; some in civilian clothes, some in uniform, like Count Spec, have planted themselves directly behind the speaker whose words rebound from this living wall like balls of light, like a fountain of fireworks.

On the left stands a man who soon attracts general attention by the peppery remarks he hurls like rockets into the midst of the assembly, flinging his opinions like hurdles in front of the rhetorical cavalry charge of the reform opponent at the desk, compelling him to halt, to answer, often exciting general amusement.

It is a man with a lion's mane of gleaming, white hair. A Henri Quatre beard of the same color on a glowing red face emphasizes his singularity. His general pose is somewhat careless, like his clothes. In spite of a somewhat belligerent air he leaves a comfortable impression upon one.

This is Adolph Hoffmann, representative of the Independent Socialists. When he stands there with his back contemptuously turned toward the speaker, he generally has his hands in his pockets. Every few minutes a deep bass gurgles up from the depths in pure Berlin jargon: " Yah, y'look like it! " and so on. Sometimes his blows tell, and the speaker must prepare for defense. In the meantime the little bell tinkles madly, and calls to order are so frequent that Adolph Hoffmann's book would soon be full if he tried to record them all. He has had venomous conflicts with Count Schwerin-Löwitz's predecessors: Jordan von Kröcher and Baron von Erffa, because they were very easily angered. Herr von Kröcher revenged himself once by saying Adolph Hoffmann was never considered as a subject of law giving, only as object. Once, before the war, after the entrance of the first Social Democrats in this, until now, pure atmosphere, when a policeman was sent for to remove Representative Borchardt who refused to listen to calls to order, Adolph Hoffmann manfully took his part.

This is Adolph Hoffman as he is and as he probably will be to the end of his life — an infamous fellow in the eyes of all lovers of order. And when he himself mounts the speaker's platform there is a regular hail storm; one strong expression after another like pea shots. Usually the Right flee from the assembly room to demonstrate their feelings. The Center follow, and the fastidious Liberals do the goose-step after them. But in the evenings, among themselves, they must have to smirk over this bombardment of words, always the same. The Free Conservative Woyna once said one must not take him too seriously; Mr. Hoffmann was the

ADOLPH HOFFMANN

original Berlin Philistine who liked to blow off to ease his mind.

Adolph Hoffmann has just reached sixty. He was born in Berlin on the sixty-first birthday of Wilhelm I, the 22d of March, 1858, just as the new period under the Prince Regent was beginning to dawn. He grew to manhood amidst the most modest circumstances, attended seven different people's schools or poor schools in four different places. At fourteen he was sent out to learn a trade; he was to have become an engraver but had to give it up on account of his eyes. He then took up gilding but did not stay long at this. He was messenger boy in a bookstore, a cloth concern, and a hardware shop, one after the other, in the meantime hiring out as a painter and gilder. In the early 90's the party called him to Halle as editor, and later to Zeitz. From 1893 on he settled down as a bookseller in Berlin and began to write. He threw overboard the ten commandments which Moses brought down from Mount Sinai, and set up ten of his own in their place. He was an atheist of the purest water; day and night he worked for his free religious ideas. For years he delivered the same speeches; once when he had uttered an especially fiery speech against the Bourgeoisie, capitalists, and class rule, he made a deep impression upon a lady listener. She soon became his wife, and, as she brought some little money with her, Hoffmann became financially independent. Another time he hurled a flaming pamphlet against the whole reactionary mass, with the intimidating title: *The Social Democrats are Coming!* — a warning to women and girls of all classes.

In time he gained some little reputation as an author and as he understood the business side, too, they soon made a place for him in the party. He always belonged to the opposition and soon became a warm friend of Stadthagen and Rosa Luxemburg, the undaunted, fanatic dogmatist. She was his little Rosie. Once at the International Socialistic Congress at Stuttgart, at a garden party, it was said that he danced a measure with the fair Rosa like a good many others of his party comrades.

He was a member of the Reichstag from 1904 to 1906. Two years, and then it was over. But he played first violin in his party, or, speaking more correctly, he beat the drum. He has ornamented the Prussian House of Representatives ever since social democracy sneaked in; that is, since 1908. He was sent from the sixth Berlin voting district, Moabit, by a small majority. In the meantime, he was candidate more than once for the Reichstag.

His parliamentary record of sins is not small. He recognized no authority, and often his jokes exceeded the limit. When occasion required he could be anti-

Semitic. When Herr von Mirbach, the Kaiser's gentleman-in-waiting, went to citizens of Jewish persuasion with his amusing begging in behalf of the Kaiser Wilhelm Memorial church, he composed an ironical ditty in the *Landtag:*

> "Peacefully passes through my mind
> Still and calm God's peace.
> Up above sits Princess Wied,
> Down below the Jews."

Mir and mich (mir — dative, mich — accusative form of the pronoun me) he mixed occasionally in his speeches. Some thought that it was intentional, others, that it was lack of education. Once when a speaker expressed the latter opinion in public, Hoffmann answered: "That's the result of your poor public schools." And the laugh was on his side.

The chapter becomes more serious when we think of the policy which led to the disruption of the party. He had thundered against participation in the election for the Prussian Landtag, but about ten years ago he allowed them to put him on the list of candidates for this same House. During the war he severely reproached the "Government Socialists" with their practical and positive labor policy; not a speech was made but what he held up the Scheidemann clique to contempt — his party comrades but yesterday. He stood at the head of the Labor Union, that group of malcontents who supported the party dogma, and among the Independent Socialists he was the Wild Man who daily swung sword and pistol against the old social democracy. He fought for the intellectual and material possession of the *Vorwärts,* and when this paper slipped from his hands, he tried in vain to found a new radical paper. He could not get permission from the Government for enough paper, but he was press corporal of the *Mitteilungs Blatt,* issued once or twice a week.

And then, on the 9th of November, 1918, came the revolution so passionately longed for. The people arose. Adolph Hoffmann raced madly in a cab all through the center of Berlin, making furious speeches on every corner. The horizon turned blood red. He gathered together twelve tried men and true, and one night when he thought no one was there, they entered and took possession of the Moss publishing house and proceeded to issue the *Berliner Volkszeitung* as the organ of the Independent Socialists, edition No. 1.

When the minister posts were passed around in the new socialistic Prussia, he assured himself of the post of Minister of Education. Together with Haenisch, leader of the majority Socialists, he took over the office on the basis of " fifty-fifty." His first official act was to advance himself a year's salary.

And then began a harlequinade. The *Deutsche Tageszeitung* smirked. When he had to sign a document or when a servant brought him the acts of the executive council he was wholly at a loss what to do. If he had not provided himself beforehand with a confidential secretary, the personal debacle would have been worse. He disgraced himself on all sides until the angels wept. But he had a passion for reform that was not to be stilled. There was no end to reform proclamations. His program looked like a kaleidoscope. With one stroke of the pen he separated state and church and calmly ordered prayers and religion to be left out of the educational system. The soul of the Catholic Center seethed. A new Kultur war was mapped out by the Catholic church. The bordering Catholic states, Upper Silesia and Rhineland-Westphalia, began to make propaganda for breaking loose from Prussia. Storm everywhere. In the midst of this general culture jamboree, Adolph Hoffmann announced in a public speech that, if the election for the National Assembly did not show a socialistic majority, the socialists would break up the Reichstag with force even if they had to bring out the machine guns again.

Herr Hoffmann had developed from a democrat to a man of force. It was high time that he laid down his "work" after seven weeks, together with the other "Independent" ministers. The former Royal Prussian Kultur could not have borne the strain much longer. The Geheimräte (privy councillors) had already threatened to strike, and the Center party was making alarming disturbances marching through the streets and demanding his scalp. But when the embittered ones forced their way into his house, Herr Hoffmann was not to be found; he had hidden himself and thus saved his precious life.

No matter how you may judge him, when you think it all over he had the courage of his convictions. More than once he was put behind the bars for libel, and that is certainly no pleasure. But the Swedish curtains did not frighten him nor change his opinions. Adolph Hoffmann remained the same old proletarian Vulcan who is comfortable only when he can spit fire and sulphur. He has lost his former influence since the day when he and his "independent" colleagues with him left the council of the people's representatives for Prussia and Germany. The ex-minister of educational and clerical affairs now has taken his place in the Reichstag among the mockers, obstructionists and scandal-makers.

XV

HELLMUT VON GERLACH

The Gerlachs have played no small rôle in the history of Prussia. They were all very conservative. Hellmut von Gerlach's grandfather was once president of police under Friedrich III; he was then an ordinary citizen, but was knighted and went to Cologne as president of the Government in 1839. His son held the same office. Hellmut gave promise of keeping up the family tradition. He studied at Jena, passed his first and second state examinations, and became assistant judge in the Landrat at Ratzeburg in the district of Sachsenwald, where the old man spent his last days grumbling and warning. Gerlach, faithful to the Government — Bismarck, bitterly opposed to the new order of things, opposed to Wilhelm II, Caprivi, Bötticher, and all the rest, in boundless contempt for Stöcker who wrote his friends in a notorious letter, that it would be a good service to the Kaiser to build a bonfire and throw old Bismarck into it. Gerlach was an absolute monarchist; Bismarck was no doubt also a monarchist, but in his passionate battle against the new régime he unintentionally became democratic. He did not stop to think that he broke the back of the Reichstag without lessening the power of the monarch a dot. This was Bismarck and Gerlach in the early 90's when they came into professional contact.

One thing Gerlach had in common with the human Vulcan: the necessity of creating an impression on politics. This desire was so strong that Hellmut began to work on Stöcker's paper, the *Volk*. He felt himself drawn to that group of Social Conservatives, or young Conservatives, which looked up to the young Tory, Randolph Churchill, as their political pattern. Gerlach believed he could reform and modernize the Conservative party socially and liberally. For this reason he fought against the socialist and all other exceptional laws. He published a vigorous article against the Reichstag when they concluded not to increase the income tax to four per cent on all incomes over 100,000 marks. On account of this article Count von der Schulenburg, Duke von Trachenberg, and other high personages, called him a socialist or even an anarchist. He was forbidden to publish any further articles or to appear in public assemblies. This was a distinction that hardly any other government barrister ever acquired. He soon became editor and gave up his official career. All at once he was in the middle of the Christian socialistic movement, writing and agitating against the Jews as "capitalistic parasites." He began to work for the social ideas of Wagner and Schmoller under the cloak of bellicose Christianity. The Conservative party admitted the justice of these demands in order to win the masses, but the people did not feel comfortable in this feudal society for any length of time; they soon saw the purpose and got in a bad humor. In 1897 they broke loose, Naumann, Göhre, and Gerlach, and founded the National Socialistic party on a platform of land reform, national socialism, and anti-Semitic culture, a somewhat hazy program. There was plenty of enthusiasm with but little practical success. It remained a party of enthusiastic officers without any troops. They could scarcely get enough under-officers together to carry on their propaganda work. Gerlach bought the *Hessische Landeszeitung* and conducted this paper from 1898 to 1906. During the first few years of his activity on this paper he continued writing leading articles for the *Welt am Montag*.

Democratic thoughts crept into his national-socialistic policy and he was soon the darling of the official world. In a certain law process a lawyer compared the *Hessische Landeszeitung* to a dirty towel on which everybody wiped his hands.

In 1903 Gerlach was candidate for the Reichstag for the first time. He won out with the help of the Center. In the meantime the National Socialistic party went to pieces on an excess of intellect. A party cannot consist entirely of speakers; there must be a few listeners as well. The Liberal organization joyfully received most of them, Gerlach included. The rest went over to the Social Democrats. In 1907, Gerlach was again candidate but lost this time. He moved to Berlin and took over the direction of the *Berliner Zeitung* in the Ullsteinhouse. Under the greatest opposition he called the democratic organization into being and struck out strongly right and left. Finally he landed in the *Welt am Montag* again and still distinguishes that paper with his Monday articles.

This is Hellmut von Gerlach's career. He is a democrat of the purest water, distilled democracy. But he lacks one thing — the inner fire which immediately impresses the reader or listener in all that he writes or says. He is a rationalist through and through. But the rationalizing of his daily life is not always correct or even reasonable. He strives to learn much of everything, loses his way and only finds it again laboriously on the path of journalism. This is a sympathetic, a kindly weakness, but nevertheless a weakness. His articles are often not penetrating enough, they are too superficial and confine themselves to mere statement of facts. He registers presumptions, assertions, proofs, builds up his thought system mathematically, therefore lacking inner "warmth and dampness," to use an expression of Xenophon's.

HELLMUT VON GERLACH

When one hears him speak or sees him write, often grinning sarcastically but always soberly consequential, one is involuntarily reminded of Pan. Every Monday morning early he suddenly pops out of the forest of everyday duties, blows his little flute admonishingly, and points out the political errors of the past week. And many buy his paper even if they are not at all democratic, and read it with curiosity and gratitude because of the liberal thoughts and continual cry for peace contained therein.

He failed utterly as under-secretary of the Prussian Ministry, to which he was appointed by the revolutionary cabinet. He was sent to Posen to report on the doings of the Poles; was completely taken in by the courtesy of the Pan-Polish National Democrats and reported everything rosy. Soon afterwards the Poles began systematically to conquer the German Ostmark in order to have a *fait accompli* for the peace conference.

XVI

KARL THEODOR HELFFERICH

Dr. Helfferich, once more, found a new sphere of activity, this time far from the Center. He was the murdered Count Mirbach's successor in Moscow. Many official and nonofficial circles in Berlin heaved a sigh of relief when he finally settled down for a time where he could not disturb with his aspirations every change of secretary or ambassador. Dr. Helfferich, personifying perpetual motion, had the pleasant task of transacting business with Bolsheviki and revolutionists between bomb fuses, so to speak. He, the most outspoken friend of capitalism, must manage to get along with the "deadly enemies of capitalism and bourgeois society." Not only this, but he must also pave the way for resuming economic relations with Russia.

Helfferich was a man who undertook much but who had no perseverance. Everything must be won at first assault. When he stood on top, a restless, fidgety person, he did not stay there long; he already cast his eye about for new fields to conquer.

He was born and grew to manhood in a house traditionally democratic. His father was a leader of the

KARL THEODOR HELFFERICH

Progressive People's party in the Palatinate. More than once the young Karl Theodor climbed upon the Hambacker Höhe where once a thousand men and women gathered in 1832, to demonstrate for freedom and a united Germany. Siebenpfeiffer saw the day coming "when Princes would exchange their feudal ermine for the manly toga of German nationality; when the German woman would no longer be the servant of the man but a free comrade of free citizens nursing their sons and daughters with the milk of freedom!" And then this gathering, full of lovely Pfalz wine, sang: "Courage, courage, courage! God will not forsake us if we keep his word in faith. Passionately let us love and passionately hate."

The next day they discussed whether a provisory Government should be established for free Germany. But this brave, and yet so pedantic, proposition was rejected. Even if this movement did come to nothing but a wine frolic, their children and children's children cherished the thought in their hearts, and if you ever visit the Palatinate it will whisper to you from every corner of the glorious days of the past. Even Karl Theodor was fascinated by the magic of it. The song of freedom filled his youthful soul. In an impetuous, poetical frenzy, he wrote a drama: "It is joy to live!" Later when he was tottering on his Vice-Chancellor throne, deserted by the Left and the Center, when he tried to support himself by turning to the Conservatives, the papers made a sarcastic allusion to his poetical gifts. This pained him so much that he notified the press through Wolff's telegraph bureau to refrain from speaking of this youthful error.

He attended the universities of Munich, Berlin and Strassburg, studying political economy. After completing his studies he made a tour of foreign lands. At twenty-three he took part in the coinage battle; naturally he was for a gold standard. At twenty-seven he entered the University of Berlin as lecturer. His career began. A shrewd, versatile, practical man, scientifically schooled, with energy and will and a full pocketbook,— not too full,— with an eye to the needs of the moment; could fate hinder the progress of such a man? A year later he was lecturing on colonial policy in the seminary for oriental languages; a year after that he found his way to the Government. He entered the colonial department of the Foreign Office. In the course of one year he was professor, Councillor of the Legation, and acting Councillor of the Legation. He was the delegate of the German Government at the Berlin transactions of the American-Mexican coinage commission. He soon acquired the reputation of being a very clever lawyer, and as he had had enough of official life, he began to work for private concerns. Financial circles had long had their eye on him. He had shown himself especially

KARL THEODOR HELFFERICH

clever and adroit as a Government commissioner in colonial transactions. At least this was the general impression; and then there was his book on money which won for him the reputation of being a keen financial man. In 1906 he entered the executive department of the Anatole Railroad Company and after two years was appointed director of the Deutsche Bank. He seemed to want to stay there longer than in other positions and waited for another day to come. And it came. He wrote new books on Germany's national wealth and the causes of the war. In January, 1915, he was asked by Bethmann-Hollweg to take over the treasury in place of Herr Kühn, who was leaving on account of poor health. At last a sphere of activity was opened to him where he could develop his whole ability and where he might accomplish great things. The press was favorable to him and in general everybody was glad that one of the most important political posts should be occupied by a man theoretically and practically trained for it.

Dr. Helfferich came, saw, and conquered, at first.

"I have taken over this office," he declared to the Reichstag in his maiden speech, "with the obligation of financing the war and keeping our financial position on a firm basis."

He raised the funds. Under his leadership almost thirty-two milliards were extorted from the people. Herr Kühn, his predecessor, had been able to raise only four and one-half milliards for the first loan. This was too little. The old bureaucratic method must be abandoned and a new propaganda system invented. Dr. Helfferich was a master at advertising; he adopted American methods to get the people to give up their money willingly. This is about the largest legacy he left behind him — bluff. On closer examination we find that nothing else will hold water.

Each war loan was almost a personal victory and yet, in the noise of triumph, one must not forget a man who played a strong part in the success of these financial schemes — Dr. Havenstein, president of the Reichsbank. When Helfferich faced the problem of a new financial system he failed miserably. Five hundred million marks were to be raised. Now was the time to unfold his genius, to develop great reform ideas. The time was favorable; but what did Helfferich do? Like a miserable ragpicker he scratched a few small taxes together and loaded them onto trade, industry and traffic. He, the economist, the financial theorist, the colonial politician!

The Reichstag was disappointed, grumbled, picked his tax bouquet to pieces, and came into conflict with him. He met the Social Democrats with the words: "I forbid you to say such things!" Naturally they only laughed at him. He could not understand why the Reichstag did not approve of his plan of taxing industrial and traffic concerns, his carefully thought-out scheme of covering the deficit. True, his arithmetic was incontestable; everything balanced. But it had its dark side. The theoretical economist had figured too abstractly — had undervalued the power of party and professional interests. This method of valuation of people and things reminds one of Colquhoun, of whom Heine relates in his *English Fragments:* "In order to give his readers an idea of the unlimited resources of the nation, he took an inventory of everything in the country down to the rabbits." Heine wittily remarks: "He seemed to regret that he could not reckon in the rats and the mice."

When the Reichstag had corrected his tax plan, replacing the indirect tax by a direct income tax, and when the Bundesrat had approved of this system, Helfferich withdrew in bad humor as if he had been personally injured. Why had he hastily declared to the Reichstag during the tax transactions: "The Governments are of the opinion that with the exception of a tax on war profiteering, any further direct national tax is impossible." Afterwards when the Government deserted him he compromised. The tax compromise was concluded without him, but he gave in gracefully because the way was already open for a higher position. Slowly he had paved the way to it. His position as Secretary of the Treasury did not satisfy him; he longed for political laurels. In his first great Reichstag speech on March 15, 1915, he declared with assurance: "It is Germany's intention to let the enemy pay for the material damage they have caused by this wanton war." A year later on another March day, he expressed the same thought but somewhat modified: "We may hope for a financially favorable peace — indeed we maintain this hope — but in spite of this an increase of national funds is very necessary." Karl Theodor had begun to learn a few things, especially about unrestricted submarine warfare. He knew how great the danger from American sources was; as a political economist he knew America's resources; her energy, material, men, and money. Although he was one of the most energetic opponents of a submarine war, he allowed himself to be won over against his better judgment like Bethmann-Hollweg, his chief. At that time he was Secretary of the Interior and Vice-Chancellor, a welcome guest at General Headquarters. This loquacious man who never lost his mental balance and always fell on his feet, made an excellent impression on the Kaiser. He soon basked in the sunlight of imperial favor, but he could not get along with the Reichstag. They did not always want what he wanted. They ventured to contradict when the great authority spoke, and spoil his concept. What did they know of the things he commanded? As head of the Department of the Interior he worked industriously to become acquainted with the new sphere, but with a sort of mimicry, an ability to fit into the old system which soon developed into a fanatical bureaucracy. He carried this autocracy into the Reichstag and this was his misfortune. Although the food department had been separated from the Department of the Interior, the new office proved too much for Dr. Helfferich. He met the problems and people with increasing nervousness; his irritability brought him into painful situations more than once.

In spite of an excess of work which threatened to swamp the office, he was at first an outspoken opponent of a division of the department, but finally accepted it, reserving the post of Vice-Chancellor for himself. He did not retain this exposed position for more than twenty-five days. The Reichstag got him out, although he fought tooth and nail against it. Herr von Payer took his place. Ajax fell by his own strength.

When one looks back over his political legacy one sees nothing but fragments. The patriotic service law introduced by him was wholly changed by the Reichstag. Only the idea remained. It was a mere accident that the Reichstag let itself be intimidated by a threat that the bill would fall through if a court of arbitration and a labor commission were forced upon the railroads. I can still see Dr. Helfferich sweating and moving restlessly back and forth on his bench. What if the majority went against him? Either the Government must withdraw the draft which was the kernel of Hindenburg's policy, or he must resign on account of his too hasty utterances. But the god Mercury was gracious. By a majority of one single vote the demands of the Left were rejected — and he was on top again. He could rub his hands with satisfaction. In his exuberance he committed the indiscretion of saying in the semi-official *Norddeutsche Allgemeine Zeitung* that he could have carried out his service law without the Reichstag's aid. Tableau. The press made a noise and Herr Helfferich retracted.

His greatest parliamentary defeat took place at the interpellation of the Pan-German propaganda in the army. Amid great uproar in the House he made the remark that no one seemed to trust him any more. No! No! was repeated so often, even by the Conservatives, that he left the speaker's platform with flapping coat-tails.

The only regulation he succeeded in putting through was that in regard to rebuilding the fleet. In spite of the Reichstag's lack of confidence Dr. Helfferich still considered himself indispensable. He had outlived Bethmann-Hollweg and Michaelis, why not Count Hertling? This intellectual profiteer had long since thrown his political principles overboard; democratic from tradition, he developed the views of the Fatherland party and finally must have had to admit to himself that he had stood on the wrong side — the course of events had changed and was running strong for the Left.

Things were quiet for a few weeks after he had been politely requested a few thousand times to leave. But only for a few weeks. He dived up again serenely from below. He refused a seat in a university as professor of political economy. He stayed in Berlin — the source of all things — and waited. After a short time he accepted a post of honor from the Chancellor, preparing for the transition period.

And then he sat in Moscow between Bolsheviki and revolutionists (after attempting to obtain Kühlmann's place in the Foreign Office) sending the worst possible news from this new, and yet so old, capital of Russia.

The ground became too hot under his feet. The German diplomatic corps retired to Pleskau behind the trenches and Dr. Helfferich brought his valuable carcass back to Berlin a tempo.

The German Philistines, the Progressives, and National Liberals could sleep peacefully once more — they had their Helfferich back again. He loathed the new order of things that followed the revolution. To be put aside became unbearable to him, so, as a sort of prelude to future reactional performances, he started a furious press-campaign against Erzberger. In the following sensational trial he was made the defendant on charges of libel and defamation of character, preferred by Erzberger. The sensation caused in Germany by the publication of the list of war criminals demanded by the Entente overshadowed for only a moment the Helfferich case. He set all Germany talking about himself, and, oh, it did his heart a lot of good.

The great trial ended. As a result Erzberger resigned from office; Helfferich paid the legal costs! Typical, in a way, of both men.

XVII

PHILIP SCHEIDEMANN

A yellowish white goatee pasted on a triangle — this is Philip Scheidemann's face — a broad, shiny path leads across the top of his large skull, with tufts of hair sticking out at the sides like the hedge along a country road. Two watery blue eyes peep calmly out of their tiny caverns. This head, which attracts attention at the first glance, rests upon a somewhat undersized body. Scheidemann has grown above the proletarian class without having acquired the allurements of the bourgeois.

He is a self-made man. Born at Cassel fifty-three years ago, he entered the people's school and learned the printer's trade like Henry George, the great American land reformer. From typesetter he advanced to proofreader and then to foreman. Finally he became a journalist. At thirty years of age he was editor of the *Mitteldeutsche Sonntags-Zeitung* in Giessen; he remained at this post for five years and then edited, one after another, the social democrat papers in Nürnberg, Offenbach, and Cassel. He settled down for some time and was elected to the Reichstag. In 1911 he became a leader of the Social Democrat party, gave up his mandate, and went to live in Berlin-Steglitz.

Once he was blood-red in his socialistic opinions, and settled at the outermost edge of the left wing of his party. He liked to speak on party days, but he was no blusterer like Zubeil, Ledebour, and Stadthagen, who went opposition at any price. With all his radicalism he always left a way open for retreat when necessary, and did not assume that hateful, personal tone when speaking of party heretics; he could also get along well with Bebel, the One and Only.

He played no small rôle in the Reichstag even before the war. At one time there was a scandal. In a speech in 1912, Schiedemann attacked the Hohenzollerns, mentioning broken promises and other similar things. Suddenly Bethmann-Hollweg arose in all his great length, gave his comrades in the Bundesrat a meaning look, and marched out with them at his heels. The Bundesrat struck. It was no novelty; in May, 1881, the same thing happened under Eugen Richter. In Scheidemann's case, the president, who had perhaps nodded a bit during the speech, did not really know what had happened for the moment. He waited until the stenogram was finished, then dutifully called for order, and the gentlemen of the Government slowly found their way back to their seats.

He was a stumbling block again in 1912, when

PHILIP SCHEIDEMANN

the new Reichstag was elected and the blue-black block (Conservative and Center, the Catholic party) suffered a defeat. This fact had to be recognized in the new majority at the presidential election. The Social Democrats were the strongest party at the election, but they agreed with the Left to choose a president from the second strongest party, the Center. Herr Spahn, president of the Supreme Court and political light of the Center, became president, Schiedemann, first vice-president, and Herr Paasche, from the National Liberals, second vice-president. Germany threatened to collapse when she found out there was a real, red Social Democrat in the presidency of the Reichstag. The papers began to rage and storm and Herr Spahn hastily resigned. One couldn't really sit on the German people's seat of honor hand in hand with a Social Democrat. A new vote was cast. Herr Scheidemann was not reëlected this time, and Germany was saved. All the political moralists went about with beaming faces. Herr Schiedemann, who had bought a brand new black coat for the occasion, wore it only one day.

Things were different during the war. Scheidemann, the Red, with diplomatic cleverness, turned over to the right side, left off his gruff opposition, and approved of the war credit and a positive labor policy. Indirectly he had a strong effect upon Bethmann-Hollweg, and from a distance vaccinated him with the teachings of democracy. Like Theodor Wolff, he immediately began to work for a compromise, a peace without annexation or compensation; he was never tired of preaching this idea. Scheidemann-peace soon became a catchword. But because he would not accept a peace at any price, because he did not fight blindly against the Government, and would not refuse the war credit, he soon came into conflict with the left wing of the House, with Haase, Bernstein, Hoffmann, and company. After stormy scenes in the Reichstag came an open breach; the "Social Democratic League" broke loose, Haase resigned and Scheidemann took his place. From this time on he had a heavy battle with the radicals in the Solingen district.

In the Reichstag he was one of the most effective speakers; he had a crisp manner of delivery with a somewhat sharp undertone. Ready of wit, he had an answer for every attack; sarcasm and humor spiced his conversation. Being elegant and smooth-tongued, he was envied by many a minister for his gift of speech. The *Vorwärts* often published his speeches.

He kept in touch with the socialists of foreign countries during the war and often went to Holland and Sweden. Whenever he packed his trunks the Conservatives, scenting trouble, began to grow uneasy.

He it was who first uttered the apt words, "pyramid of skulls" and "fools who still believed in a military

PHILIP SCHEIDEMANN

victory." It was due to his clever political tactics that the Reichstag majority was formed which put an end to the dismembered condition of the Reichstag from which the Right profited so much. He entered the people's Government as Secretary of State, together with Groeber, Erzberger, Haussmann, and Friedberg, the quintet headed by Prince Max von Baden. He it was who proclaimed the new Social Republic from the balcony of the Reichstag on the 9th of November. As a decisive and strong man he played no small rôle in Ebert's revolutionary cabinet; together with the Secretary for Foreign Affairs he was chosen leader of the peace commissioners.

When on February 6, 1919, the revolutionary council of people's representatives placed their portfolios in the hands of the National Assembly, Schiedemann entered the Cabinet formed by the three democratic parties, the Democrats, the Catholic Centrists and the old Social Democrats, as Prime Minister. But his new glory, propped up largely by parliamentary rhetorics, could not last long. When the unexpectedly severe terms of the peace treaty became known, Schiedemann, after some wavering, finally said "Never!" and declared that "the hand that signs this peace ought to rot." The peremptory "Either — Or" of the Entente finished the Schiedemann Cabinet. There was nothing for him to do but to resign. He went to Switzerland for some months. While still there, he was tendered the chairmanship of the Committee on Foreign Relations which he accepted, and shortly after his return to Germany his Cassel speech rang like a trumpet blast throughout the country, warning the new German republic of the ever-present and steadily growing menace of a counter-revolution by the militarist and reactionary parties and elements, a prediction which events seem to have justified. At the beginning of 1920 he was elected First Mayor of the City of Cassel, where he was born.

From printer's boy to minister and Excellence — one has heard of like cases in America.

XVIII

HERMANN PAASCHE

Not only serious political conversations are carried on in the imposing vaulted lobby of the Reichstag; nor are mere economic questions the sole subject of discussion. No, it is here that real business is done, or better, prepared. In bluish cigar-smoke and comfortable leather chairs, it is discussed just as it is everywhere else in the masculine world. The atmosphere is much too masculine since general secretaries and recorders began to increase like the sands of the sea among parliamentarians; since trusts, syndicates, associations, and gigantic business firms are sending their representatives to the Reichstag. Every tiny business concern seeks a connection with the outer world through a representative. Lately I was asked if I knew some comrade, some "representative of the people" who would take over an easy position with a syndicate. For a reasonably high salary he was to establish and cultivate "relations." Others belong to one, two, three, or more boards, according to their reputation and position in the party.

Of course there are strictly honorable men in the Reichstag and Landtag, who are merchants or financial men and members of boards, whom no one can reproach for misusing or abusing their position. But there are others for whom the border line is blurred, who half-unconsciously make business of politics and politics of business. One became an adept at this and that was Hermann Paasche, vice-president of the Reichstag. Here is a whole ball of yarn to untangle.

Papers and pamphlets have long made biting remarks about Herr Paasche's commercial politics, but they did not venture to publish a lot of details which would serve to give us a life-size portrait of this business politician. I will try to make good the deficiency, but must confess beforehand that I cannot exhaust the topic nor expose all of Herr Paasche's doings because some of them are not yet finished.

He is somewhat above the average height, slightly stooped, and wears a filthy, black overcoat. When one sees him carelessly shambling along, or hears him bubbling like a soda-water fountain for hours at a time, when one looks into his twinkling, good-natured, little, black-currant eyes bedded in his comfortable, round face — one cannot believe what one hears of him behind the scenes. This good-natured old uncle of sixty-eight, who still looks as if he just came from the farm!

Hermann Paasche was an agrarian in his younger years and still is on a large scale. He generally retired to his beautiful estate, "Waldfrieden," by Hochzeit in

HERMANN PAASCHE

Neumark, to rest from his political exertions. This was Wilhelm Bruhn's election district, with whom Paasche was on the best of terms. In Halle he studied political economy; in 1877 he went to Aix-la-Chapelle as lecturer, and then to Rostock as professor. Against the will of the faculty he went to Marburg; Althoff, the Allpowerful from the Ministry of Education, favored him and half forced him upon the university. About this time his parliamentary career began, but on account of his leaving Mecklenburg in 1884, he had to give up his Mecklenburg mandate. He kept away from politics for nine years. Then he was sent to the Diet from Meiningen and represented Kreuznach-Simmern in the Reichstag.

As professor he was not very highly treasured. I do not know of one student who looked up to him as a teacher — I know only of those who covered their ears and shuddered when they thought of the cataract of words that poured from his mouth. He would give the contents of whole books in forty-five minutes, but I am sure there was more quantity than quality. His literary works consisted of insignificant publications on various subjects. One seeks in vain for original ideas; they are mere statements of facts and statistics. There are a few travel sketches among them of trips to North and Central America, to Jamaica and Cuba. A few years before the war he was also in East Africa. Writing was not his field; his talents were bent in another direction. He settled down on the periphery of business life and soon attained the success denied him as a scholar. He obtained a good position in the National Liberal party. He had economic problems to deal with as his special territory, and soon became an authority on such things in the party. Government men crowded about him and new relations and business connections were formed. Industrial firms who largely depend upon Government orders, or firms interested in the outcome of a tax or tariff law, fought for his protection. Little by little he became:

President of the Board of Howaldt's Works.

Board member of the:

    German Mineral Oil Industry, A. G.

    German-Bohemian Coal and Pressed Coal Works, A. G. in Dresden.

    Brewery, Alcohol, and Yeast Works, formerly G. Skinner, Smelter Works, C. Wilh. Kayser & Co., A. G.

    Rhineland Metal and Machine Factory.

    Rositzer Sugar Refinery, A. G.

    Telephone Factory, A. G., formerly J. Berliner.

Is that all? These are not all by any means, only the largest firms are mentioned here. There are all sorts of shady and shadier transactions, but I shall mention only a few which best represent Herr Paasche, the great National Liberal patriot and representative of the people.

Before the war when Americans were contemplating drawing the German cigarette industry into the combine, for some unknown reason he took the part of the firms who had entered the American trust and fought against the anti-trust League. Again we see him on the side of the foreigners when a number of foreign moving-picture concerns, Gaumont, Eclair, Cines, etc., sought to form a combine which would have ruined the German picture industry. The day was saved by the Paris firm, Pathé Frères, who refused to enter the combine.

During the war, of course, Dr. Paasche confined his activities to German allies; he played a leading rôle in the Austrian-Hungarian economic league, edited the *Wirtschaftszeitung* for the Central powers, had his hand in the German-Austrian-Hungarian railway concern, made frequent trips to Vienna, Budapest, and Sofia, permitted himself to be decorated with orders (except in Constantinople, where admittance was refused him), and always spoke for the whole German nation.

How can a man accomplish all this — politics and business and representation, day in, day out, for twelve or fourteen hours a day every day?

I shall attempt to explain the riddle. Do you happen to know Georg Kaiser's "Coral," a play given by Reinhardt last winter? It is the story of a man, a multimillionaire (which Paasche has not yet become), who is so much taken up with social and professional duties that he divides his ego with his secretary who carries on half of his burdens with all their responsibilities and obligations. Herr Paasche's other ego was not a private secretary, but contented himself with being called Syndikus. Originally he was a clerk in the Austrian-Hungarian consulate at Berlin, where he had the political business problems to look after. As Herr Paasche's other self, he had a stately income.

This gentleman looked after Herr Paasche's affairs and prepared the way for other profitable relations or for new Board memberships. For his trouble he received cash or papers — for each separate enterprise. When Herr Paasche entered a new Board he immediately complained of overwork and his other self took over the representation as far as possible.

I must break off although there is much more to be said. For instance, Herr Paasche was interested in a publishing concern which speculated on the vanity of its subscribers and advertisers — but we will be silent. The president of the German House of Representatives must keep up appearances.

He retired quickly when the new revolutionary Germany stepped forward and announced through the press that he would not accept a candidacy for the National Assembly.

XIX

HANS DELBRÜCK

A conservative but not a Heydebrand type was Hans Delbrück, a Kultur-conservative, combining all the elements of Prussia — that is, of liberal Prussia as she was in the period between the battles of Jena and Leipzig; a politician ever striving after the truth but unable to rise above his nature, whose conservatism was like a magnet ever pulling his thoughts back from their highest flights. He was a prisoner within himself. He wavered between two generations; hesitated on the bridge between the old and the new Prussia; like Lot's wife he could not resist glancing backward. He wanted to cheer up those remaining behind and hold back those who were pressing forward; his lively temperament drew him on with those at the front, but critical reason always pulled the check-rein in time.

This was the tiny, bearded, Professor Hans Delbrück, just seventy years old, historian at the University of Berlin. The name Delbrück often appears on the pages of Prussian history during the last century. Most of the Delbrücks were persons above the average — Berthold, Rudolf, Clemens. Berthold, the father, who was judge of the court of appeals in Greifswald, made little impression upon the children because of his early death.

It was the mother who gave most to the children intellectually. She was the daughter of the philosopher, von Hennig, who once worked on the theory of colors with Goethe and was later Hegel's most fluent apostle. He enjoyed much mental stimulation within professorial circles in Greifswald, even as a student. The scholars lived wholly in the atmosphere prepared by Goethe and Hegel; there were but a few who allowed the cool draft of stormy, young, literary Germany — Heine, Börne, Gutzkow, Freytag — to reach this still corner.

Delbrück wanted to become a teacher at first, but a friend of his mother's, the historian Karl von Noorden, pointed out another way. Instead of taking his examinations at Greifswald he went to Bonn and entered Sybel's school. He worked his way through tediously on contributions from two uncles, and then took up an academic career. A thousand hindrances made the road difficult. For five years he served the Crown Prince Friedrich as tutor of the young Prince Waldemar. In 1881 he became lecturer at the University of Berlin. He waited fifteen years for a post as professor. This was in 1896 and Delbrück was forty-eight years of age. It was bitter for a scholar who had long since made a reputation through his publications.

During the war I went to Skierniwice where once three Kaisers met in the gleaming white hunting lodge;

where Bismarck, with Giers and Kalnoky, laid down Europe's program for a decade. I was guest of the district leader, a conservative Reichstag representative. The Count, Major of the Brown Hussars, was a splendid example of jovial Junker with his patriarchal impudence. We were sitting with cigars and cognac when he surprised me by taking a blue volume from the writing table, with the remark: "Look here, this has been my reading-matter for years." It was the *Preussisches Jahrbuch,* started by Treitschke, now published by Delbrück after forty years. To see a genuine Prussian Junker diligently studying politics was a great surprise. I believed Delbrück to be thrown out altogether from these circles — Delbrück who had sat on the benches of the Free Conservatives! He still had credit with the Right it seemed! Although he had always been opposed to discriminating laws against the Danes, the Poles, and Alsatians, although it was he who unmasked the shyness of the landed property owner in regard to taxes, although he was a Bethmann-Hollweg man during the war and a bitter opponent of the Alldeutschers (Pan-German) there must have been something in this little political professor to attract the stiffest Conservative. Probably this attraction was Prussian militarism.

What had he to do with militarism? Surely he was Lieutenant of the reserves during the war of 1870–71; everybody was in arms at that time. It was nothing extraordinary. But his special subject was the history of war. It was here that he did something extraordinary. He went back into antiquity and proved step by step, from the Persian wars, the transmission of the art of war and army formations. Here was much that was not understood, much that was legendary, and there was no one to show him the path out of this wilderness. His fundamental work was the Gneisenau biography. In this work he treats of strategy and methods then employed to defeat the enemy. From his *History of the Art of War,* Schlieffen got his idea for the battle of Cannae.

His military articles in the *Preussische Jahrbücher* on different phases of the late war are most enjoyable. From month to month the military events are analyzed in clear language and dignified consequence. The political street of knowledge was not so broad and smooth for him. For example, when one reads his book *War and Politics,* one stumbles upon many mistakes and misses the sure hand that is necessary to guide one out of the political chaos of the day.

Although he fought for equal suffrage he cannot free himself of the old, Liberal-Conservative, Prussian narrowness of the days following 1848. But I respect him as teacher and politician, for his writings and his personality. And I love Hans Delbrück's temperament and admire his courage.

XX

THEOBALD VON BETHMANN-HOLLWEG

The publications from the Bavarian archives, on the question of who is to blame for the war loosed von Bethmann-Hollweg's tongue. He sought to justify his policy and suggested an investigation by the Supreme Court. It was a confession of his weakness. The events of that time were too much for him.

Who and what was Herr von Bethmann-Hollweg? He had almost been forgotten in the confusion of political events when suddenly his long, thin form rose up again from oblivion.

We have to think hard to get back to the days of Prussian national authority. When Bethmann-Hollweg was placed at the head of the Government by the Kaiser in 1909, he had to wade through a mountain of political débris to reach the Chancellor's palace. The authority of the Government, which had just solemnly declared it would not accept the finance reform without an inheritance tax, was badly undermined. It had to bend under the Caudinian yoke of the blue-black (Conservative and Catholic center) block. Prince Bülow's parliamentary working majority had gone to pieces, the Center again set the pace and a savage party battle began. A financial reform that made deep wounds in their economical life was forced upon the German people. Trade, industries, and business concerns formed a league against the one-sided, selfish, economical tendencies of the agrarian Conservatives. Never was Germany in the throes of such an inner convulsion as then.

Herr von Bethmann-Hollweg warned the representatives to creative work in his first speech. No nation, he said, could hold its breath forever while sensational party quarrels were being hashed over. That would kill the nerve of any nation; her faith in herself and her position in the world would be ruined. A nation like Germany who won her place in the world by sober work, could keep it only by continuing to work. He was convinced that there was a necessity for creation laid upon every member of the nation, and that this necessity would outlive the present state of confusion.

But his warning fell on deaf ears. The inner battle went on until 1912, when the new Reichstag election opened the valve. The whole Left was now so strong that they formed the majority, if it were but a small one. In those two and a half years of battle Bethmann-Hollweg had tried to accomplish a number of urgent tasks. He slowly approached the Center which had declared him to be but a "temporary Chancellor." The battle of the Vatican against the liberal tendency creeping into the church, the oath laid upon numerous scientific men, which was an infringement upon the rights of the state, created so much disturbance among the people that the Government had to interfere in some way. Bethmann-Hollweg approached the task gingerly. The ghost of a Kultur war haunted him but still he tried to come to a compromise with the Vatican. He also took the first hesitating steps toward a discussion of the Jesuit problem. His restraint in the Ostmark question, his reluctance to use the expropriation law, his attempt to reconcile the Polish nobility after a decade of estrangement by the arrangement of the Kaiser's visit to Posen, and the liberal constitution he gave Alsace-Lorraine, strengthened his position with the Center from day to day. This policy of compromise brought him gradually into conflict with the Right; his attitude toward foreign affairs did not serve to better this condition. One thing after another came to widen the cleft between them: Alsace-Lorraine, the Prussian franchise problem, the Zabern affairs, and the profiteers' tax as a substitute for the inheritance tax. In spite of it all, he took great pains to give the preference to this circle in every way possible.

At last the Left began to mistrust him. The election reform he contemplated introducing served to deepen the chasm now formed between him and the Liberals. The words he used in introducing the bill made an understanding almost impossible. He said one's whole life consisted of dependencies, dependencies erected by God. But Bethmann did not give up trying to come to an understanding with them, and indeed he succeeded shortly before the war in bringing the Left, and even the Social Democrats, to his standard, although when the second military bill was introduced they rejected the army bill and profiteer tax. This made a great impression on foreign countries.

In the meantime Bethman-Hollweg's foreign policy was conducted with ever-increasing difficulties. When he entered the Chancellor's office he was new to diplomacy. Instinctively he was led by the thought of gradually loosening the meshes of the English-French-Russian net cast around Germany. As in Bismarck's case, the coalition nightmare caused him many a sleepless night. He began with Russia, with Sassanow. The Potsdam interview and agreement in regard to Persia and the Bagdad railroad seemed to create a better feeling. The attempt to come to an understanding with England also seemed promising in the beginning. But Haldane's visit to Berlin led to a new dissonance; von Tirpitz was the cause. New threads were spun, new prospects opened up. The Crown Prince was discontented but Bethmann-Hollweg went his own way. Then the storm broke; war could no longer be avoided. The Kaiser's generals dictated with the sword and tore up the treaty

THEOBALD VON BETHMANN-HOLWEG

with Belgium. Bethmann-Hollweg protested — but remained in office preaching to the Reichstag that the wrong should be righted.

During the war he felt the approaching calamity more and more clearly from day to day and warned them to come to terms. In 1915 he declared himself agreeable to a League of Nations, but the Alldeutschers the Conservatives despised him as a weakling and idealist. Then came the agitation for an unrestricted submarine warfare. Pamphlets shot up like mushrooms over night; a Pan-German secret court-martial was held and the verdict was: "We've got to get rid of that fellow!" But Bethmann-Hollweg held out against them. Tirpitz was removed from office and yet — one day Helfferich left him in the lurch and got up new statistics which made a submarine war appear imperative. Bethmann-Hollweg was voted down at the conference at Headquarters. The U-boat war was proclaimed in the midst of America's endeavor to bring about peace. But he remained in office although the Alldeutschers were better pleased than before.

He won the Social Democrats to his side in this war for the existence of the nation — they gave up their class standpoint, the Independent organizations placed themselves at the service of the Government, and the German people presented a united front to the foe. But Bethmann did not know how to take advantage of this situation. True, he had learned something from this inner rejuvenation he was always talking about. He became absorbed in the ideals of democracy, but his thoughts never developed into deeds. The only practical thing he did was, here and there, to clear the way for proficiency; he did not hesitate to put even organized Social Democrats in office if they could fill the job. Otherwise he contented himself with repealing the laws in regard to foreign languages and youths, also the Jesuit law. His Easter message and promise of equal suffrage were the last attempts to soothe the spirits of democracy. Schmoller once called him a modern Fabius Cunctator. He was filled with the best intentions, he saw the necessity of reorganizing Prussia's antiquated system, but never found the way to deeds. He overrated the opposition and fell at last because his indecisive policy could go no further. He was forsaken by the Center he had made love to for so long; the National Liberals followed and he lost his parliamentary support.

Curiously enough he could be decisive when it came to getting rid of persons who might be dangerous to him. This was the case in the change of ministers which cost Baron von Rheinbaben his place, and in the quarrel with Tirpitz. Personal relations were an important factor in his political calculus. Not once, but many times, he sent confidential persons — principally scientific men — to announce from the lecture platform what he later intended to do. He also used the press — and used it very cleverly.

There were many surprises concealed in this man who had a purely bureaucratic career behind him. He began as Landrat in Niederbarnim, became president of Potsdam, and then Minister of the Interior, finally Secretary of the Interior, successor to Count Posadowsky. Bethmann-Hollweg liked to emphasize the ethical streak in his policy. People said he had a liking for philosophy; in his idle hours he studied Kant and Schopenhauer and the music of Brahms. One still remembers the stir his words created when he once said: "Our philosophy has slowly recognized Kant, that great, mental aristocrat!"

This was Bethmann's philosophy, but it was not sufficient to have willed the best — in politics one must have also accomplished the best. He began too late and — fell. He had won over the Kaiser entirely for his reform ideas; he had caused the resignation of opposing ministers, but when von Stein, Minister of War, declared himself an opponent of equal suffrage, Ludendorff declared that without von Stein he would not be responsible for the command of the army.

The catchword became: Bethmann or Ludendorff?

And Bethmann fell when he thought himself the securest.

XXI

MINNA CAUER

Among those publishers who are known by their works are a few women. They are all militant natures who take everything with deadly seriousness and who have not yet acquired a rational polish. Men who write for the day are mostly skeptics; they gradually realize that their wares are not worth much more than the paper they are written on. But women who have once entered the public arena are to the last breath mental Amazons who plunge into the battle anew each day with a shout of victory on their lips. And they are right — those who conquer life anew hour for hour, those who enter into the thing with their whole souls, who give their very existence for the principle. The others follow, drawn by suggestion.

One can count on one's fingers the women in public life who have anything worth saying, although two generations have participated in the feminist movement. One of the best, Lady Braun, a female Vulcan, has gone to rest after decades of activity. In the midst of her most intensive work a remorseless God called her home. A part of the way she wandered with Minna Cauer.

MINNA CAUER

In the 90's, when German intelligence was enthusiastic over the socialist movement, she married the scholar, von Gyzicki, and together they published *Ethische Kultur,* at a time when idealists were listening to the words of Moritz von Egidy: " Religion is no longer a thing apart; our life itself is religion."

Minna Cauer is already in her seventy-eighth year. A veteran? She would laugh at you if you approached her respectfully as if she were a walking arteriosclerosis. She is young mentally and physically; intellectually as nimble as a weasel. Where the battle rages wildest there you will find her. Her life has been like a movie-film — ever changing and shimmering, much sorrow but also much success. She is always driven forward by the ideals, freedom, social and political equality for women.

Freedom! That reminds one of her first revolutionary prank. She was seven years old when the unrest of 1848 crept into quiet little Freyenstein in Ostpriegnitz, where her father, Herr Schaller, was pastor. At the head of a troop of boys and girls she marched through the streets singing revolutionary songs and waving flags. Of course father scolded, but Minna kept on treading the path of freedom. For a time she did as other girls did — entered a boarding school and when she was twenty-one she bestowed her hand upon a young doctor, August Latzel. This marriage lasted four years, during which time she lost a little son of two years and her husband, who came home ill from the campaign against Denmark in 1864, to die soon after — the fate of many a woman — a widow still young and fresh, good for a lifetime, and yet discouraged and uprooted. She went to Paris as a governess, saw all the great men at the height of their glory, Napoleon and Eugenie — all the intoxication of the second Empire. Months later when the war cast her back upon German shores, this seemed like a dream. The splendid, glittering, Napoleonic soap-bubble had burst.

Minna married again. She accepted a position in Hamm as teacher in a girls' school, and married the director of the Gymnasium, a widower with five children, a historian of some little repute, Professor Eduard Cauer. They went to Danzig and then to Berlin. Kaiser Friedrich (then Crown Prince) and his wife interested themselves in the young couple. Often they exchanged opinions. After twelve years Minna lost her second husband. Again her life must be wholly rearranged. Hesitatingly she began to enter public life. From long association with her husband she became interested in history. After his death, in looking over his diary she found this passage: "The history of woman is not yet written; it must be written sometime but it will require the devotion of a lifetime." Was fate pointing out the way?

MINNA CAUER

Frau Cauer wrote little historical sketches but this was only a side line. The present took hold of her and the past sank into oblivion. A few liberal men who had founded a German Academic Verein now proposed a woman's organization. After long persuasion Minna Cauer took over the leadership in 1888. At the first general meeting she announced that it was not to be a club which was to be contented with mere existing; no, it should spread the women's movement far and wide and prepare the soil for its reception. At the same time she was mapping out her own career to which she remained true the rest of her life. Together with Lily von Gyzicki and Adele Gerhard, she sent the first petition to the Reichstag asking for the right to organize women's political vereins. "Three women citizens" mocked the Social Democrats. Only in 1908 was this wish fulfilled.

In the meantime she continued her work, devoting herself to the interests of shop-girls; she founded an Aid Society and took part in founding the League of Women's Clubs. It is impossible to mention all of her activities in this short sketch. For ten years she had devoted herself almost exclusively to the battle for equal suffrage, equal political rights.

Her thoughts have been published since 1895 in the *Frauenbewegung*. Numberless are her articles, political, social, and cultural. There is nothing dry or theoretical about them; they are living and scintillating, they flash into the mind of the reader. She will hear nothing of Society Welfare organizations. That is play — work is the need of the hour, daily, hard, social work. When the war broke out she was one of the first to lend her aid to the Red Cross. For a year and a half she did her duty in Berlin; saw behind the scenes more than she wished to see; observed with disfavor the chase after Orders and other marks of distinction. When they tried to catch her with one of these " ribbons " she left and again devoted herself to political things.

She draws a large line between herself and the " charitable lady." Once she wrote: " There is a deep cleft in the world of women to-day. An ocean of opinions separates us from those who are rooted in aged conventionalities. There are new problems to solve and they are not easy ones. To be sure, it is more comfortable to cling to that which is old and adore it. Carlyle speaks of the old clothes of history; we do not feel ourselves called upon either to wear them or to patch them."

The battle for equal suffrage in Prussia gave new impetus to her efforts. Now it was everything or nothing. She appeared again and again on the platform, spoke to thousands; forged the women's organizations into a solid phalanx for the approaching battle, sent a deputation of women to ask the intentions of the members of the Reichstag. When the great election reform was finally put through, there was nothing said about the women. They were glad to get equal suffrage for the men. But even this defeat did not discourage Minna Cauer; she went on speaking, writing, agitating, with her heart's blood — this youthful woman of seventy-seven. The revolution brought her the fruits of victory. A woman's life was rounded out.

XXII

PAUL LENSCH

Forty-five years ago his parents baptized him with the name of Paul. His mother insisted on it; all mothers have a fine instinct, and besides, her own name was Pauline. She foresaw what would become of the wild, fidgety Paul and she was not mistaken.

Paul was born at Potsdam in the shadow of the great Friedrich, three years after the Franco-Prussian War. Wilhelm I and Friedrich III, Bismarck and Moltke, heroes whose laurel wreaths were just beginning to fade, glided past his cradle.

Prussian-German history was hammered into him at the Havel gymnasium while drums were beating outside on the parade grounds where the soldiers were being drilled. In this way he received a firm, concrete basis to work on, so to speak. When this was over he entered the university. In Berlin and Strassburg he studied political economy. Hegel, Marx, and Lassalle, Wagner, Schmoller, and Brentano fascinated him; greedily he devoured the teachings of that great socialistic church-father, Kautsky. Although he served in the fourth regiment of the Guards for a year, there was no stopping him on the way to socialism now. In 1900 he was promoted to Doctor of Political Science at Strassburg; immediately afterwards he became editor of the *Freie Presse für Elsass-Lothringen*.

As an author he is hesitating, doctrinaire, but not class-conscious. Trips abroad widened his horizon. Finally he landed in Leipzig, where there seemed a chance of making a living. Rosa Luxemburg had beckoned; Rosa, the morning star of the party, editor of the *Leipziger Volkszeitung*. Lensch did not let himself be asked twice; as early as 1902 we saw him buzzing around the editor's room. Here at the cradle of German socialism he became more radical than ever. Franz Mehring wrote the much admired historical articles for the paper, although he was forbidden to enter the locality — no one could get along with him, not even Kautsky. Jaeckh took Rosa's place and published those traditional sow-herd articles which were to distinguish the paper from that time on. Lensch was in his element — when Mehring somewhat sarcastically reproached him with being lazy he gradually began to liven up his articles. Very soon there was no one more radical, more savage, more insubordinate than he. The poor bourgeois were mauled, beaten, struck dead with ink; with haughty mien he planted his class-conscious, revolutionary foot on the necks of the reactionary masses. The proletariat was pictured with an aureole around its head. He spoke in this fashion to hundreds of public gatherings, and the resolutions he proposed were dipped in the gore of the red Internationale.

But the poor weavers of Saxony and Thüringen were still some distance from him in spite of his swashbuckling radicalism. For no matter how wildly he gesticulated he could not deny the academic streak in his veins. In spite of this the Saxon district Reichenbach-Auerbach sent him to the Reichstag. He did not make much of a stir there. When he made his first speech some wag called from the reporters' bench: "At last we have a rhyme for Mensch (people), Mr. Lensch." He was not a big number on party days either; was known only as Mrs. Rosa's cavalier, whose teachings he raved over. With his slouch Panama hat perched cockily on one side, his mustache curled up on the ends, generally wearing a gray suit — gray like his theory — he was the cavalier of the party. He usually led a dog on a strap and loved to quote from books — in these respects he resembled a converted Bülow. This radical Bülow was an abomination to Frank, Landsberg, and Bernstein; they ostentatiously avoided his society. They didn't even speak in passing. In 1908 he became editor of the *Leipziger Volkszeitung.*

This was Paul Lensch before the war. In class-consciousness he was not to be out-trumped even by Liebknecht or his consorts. The mills of the gods grind slowly we all know — his hour came somewhat suddenly. The God of the middle class gathered up their prodigal son, led him back to the paths of virtue and respect for those who govern here as well as in heaven, back to love of his country and the Fatherland party. At first he flared up mightily when war broke out and spluttered with the party against war credit. When everyone else was in the first stages of war intoxication he was steadfast and unflinching. But somewhere, somehow, came the illumination. Youth and Potsdam traditions knocked at his heart; the scales fell from his eyes. Quickly he changed his shirt — pulled off the international one and donned the national. From this hour on he was the Social Imperialist of the party who was not even averse to annexation provided it were baptized with a less embarrassing name.

Of course he could not stay on the *Leipziger Volkszeitung* any longer. Together with Heilmann he founded a new mouthpiece, *Die Glocke*. Naturally he tried to justify this change of heart. His new creed was laid down in a book called *Social Democracy: Its End and its Prosperity,* published by S. Hirzel in Leipzig. The reasoning procedure was certainly not easy to follow, but a student of Hegel, who can play with dialectics as with a billiard ball, can accomplish even this.

Thus spoke Lensch: " The principle of the organization, which in the hands of public authorities means as much as guardianship, police surveillance, and submission on the part of the subject, will then become the dialectic opposite — will be the lever of self-government and discipline as soon as it becomes a part of the masses themselves." He closes this play of words with: "At the head of the German revolution stands Bethmann-Hollweg."

We others, who are not so schooled in dialectics, have not yet been able to see it that way; on the contrary we have found public authority mightier than ever during the war, and submission on the part of the subject has already entered the blood of nurslings on account of bread, milk, and meat cards.

Herr Lensch's mental pendulum has swung over to the other side and he has had a good many credulous followers. Miracles happen even to-day; if you believed they happened only in biblical times just take a look at Dr. Solf's exclusive and distinguished *German Society of 1914,* and there you will find Herr Lensch comfortably ensconced in a leather chair every evening.

In one hour Saul became Paul.

XXIII

ERNST GRAF ZU REVENTLOW

Not all Pan-Germans are alike — of course not. There are a thousand variations ranging from three octaves in the bass to three in the treble, to express it musically. The strongest note is struck by Count Ernst zu Reventlow, who speaks daily to the public through the medium of the *Deutsche Tageszeitung*. He is a remarkable creature. There is not a human instinct he does not touch upon — not a contradiction in which he does not entangle himself. A smooth dialectic is all that saves him.

This sophist once took unto himself a French woman for a wife; for her sake he retired from the army. The companion he won at such heavy price stands by his side to-day. They went to Central America and tried ranching but it was not a success. Disappointed, they turned back to the Fatherland. That was almost twenty years ago. Then he tried his hand at writing. We first meet him in *Überall,* an illustrated army and navy paper. Then he became marine specialist for the *Berliner Tageblatt,* and some time afterwards he landed on the *Tägliche Rundschau,* where his first anti-

Semitic utterances appear. But he was still a liberal-minded man, although not attached to any particular party program. He attacked Tirpitz, who stood at the head of the navy bureau — even the Kaiser was not immune. About 1907 a booklet appeared entitled, *The Kaiser and the Byzantine.* His Majesty surrounded himself only with flatterers, he wrote, and related a merry episode. On a hunting trip to England, when Wilhelm II bagged a large number of animals, a chubby-cheeked English country gentleman sarcastically exclaimed: "Almost superhuman." He also criticized Prince Heinrich in the *Tägliche Rundschau* because he drilled his sailors on horseback and performed other comical feats unbecoming an Admiral of the Navy. Imagine a galloping mounted navy!

But no one rapped his fingers for his naughtiness, and many giggled to themselves over this noble *enfant terrible*. But one day his foot slipped — he criticized the Potsdam cavalry — said they didn't do as much as the ordinary infantry. This was too much. They haled him before a court of honor. There was a painful process in which all the rest of his literary sins were taken into account. The verdict was: Guilty; the prosecution recommended depriving him of his title and uniform. This was disgrace and shame for an officer. But the sentence was somewhat milder; he was allowed to retain his title but was retired from service.

ERNST GRAF ZU REVENTLOW

This was his day of enlightenment; the purging of the hero began. If you like we can name the very day of his change of spirit — the 14th of March, 1908. He saw the world and all things therein with new eyes. He began to applaud Tirpitz whom he had formerly so frequently attacked. Thereupon Tirpitz smilingly declared that Reventlow was his favorite literary mariner. One door after another was opened to him in the Navy Department. Every hour they put interesting material into his hands; he needed only to utter the wish. In the meantime, through Dr. Rösicke's friendly interference, he went over to the *Deutsche Tageszeitung*. He liked this journalistic, demagogic platform much better — it suited his nature. With all their Teutonic propensities, they handled politics with kid gloves on in the Zimmerstrasse. Here, on the *Deutsche Tageszeitung,* he could handle them with a dung fork if occasion demanded, without insulting his readers' nostrils with the stirred-up odor. At first he confined himself to marine politics, but his was a commanding nature. He soon became irritating to the comfortable Herr Oertel, the Christian standard bearer of the Landowners' League and editor-in-chief of the *Deutsche Tageszeitung*. They jarred on each other's nerves. But one day they carried Herr Oertal's remains out to God's acre, and Reventlow's power was thenceforth undisputed. Mornings and evenings he wrote a leading article; navy problems formed but one chapter. He wrote on home and foreign politics, cultural questions, anti-Semitism, in short, everything; and he will keep on writing morning, noon, and night. The language of these rabbit-like productions is fearful. There are sentences whose backbone is broken a half dozen times; there are miracles of style compared with which the excrescences of the baroque period are mere trifles; there is a confusion of contradictions, scurrilous notions, and psychological impossibilities. Thoughts revolve like arabesques around a few old prejudices, idiosyncrasies, and abstract conceptions; an eternal monotony, covered by a scholarly dialectic which appears charming to some. His book, *Germany's Foreign Policy, 1888–1914,* had its good qualities in spite of its untrustworthiness.

The things he fought for were but a heap of false conceptions. In his battle for the increase of the navy, he occupied himself with the submarine question even before the war. In 1908 he hurled reproaches at Tirpitz for not competing with England in the building of submarines. "It is a shame," he wrote, "that Germany has but one such boat." Afterwards, during the war, when he had begun to protect Herr von Tirpitz, he declared all at once: "It is a mistake to speak of shirking submarine construction." His predictions were no less contradictory than the use of the weapon itself. In 1909, he did not value the submarine as a weapon very highly. "The German torpedo boat," he wrote, "can only penetrate the broad girdle of England's system of defense if she is protected. For this purpose our whole fleet is necessary under certain circumstances. The feasibility of such warfare rests upon our fleet." It was just the other way about as we have seen. The fleet stayed at home and the accomplishments of the torpedo and U-boats exceeded the expectations of the most fantastic-minded at first. But enough of the marine question.

He blustered around still more dangerously in foreign politics where he broke many a window with his rhetorical stones. He had no consideration whatever, no feeling of responsibility, no psychological restraints. After the storm broke over Europe he began to work for the most extensive annexations: Belgium, especially the coast of Flanders, parts of France, Calais and other coast towns, Courland, Lithuania; and milliards of money and raw stuffs as indemnities were absolutely necessary for Germany's existence. Whoever dared to differ with him — and there were a few such reflective persons — was immediately denounced as unpatriotic. He barked continually at Bethmann-Hollweg's heels, like a yapping terrier. He fairly rained suspicions and libels upon leading statesmen, even went so far as to threaten them. "Petty, shilly-shally, spineless," were some of his tenderest epithets for the Chancellor during the discussion of the American question.

Herr Reventlow had never believed in an American declaration of war; he had always written that Germany should not let herself be bluffed by America. When it came to war he laughed contemptuously at the seriousness with which certain circles regarded the affair. To hear him talk one would believe America had no political influence whatever with the Entente, and that she could not land three soldiers on the European continent. This was entirely false, as Germany learned to her sorrow. Things might have gone otherwise had she not had America for an enemy. This saber-rattling patriotism which was always awaiting the moment when England would be crushed, created some disorder in the Count's ethics.

He called the Zeppelin attacks on England a beneficial compensation for the German answer to the Pope's note. "We cannot imagine a more joyful accompaniment." Another time he sought to reconcile hate and revenge with the teachings of Christianity.

This was Count Reventlow. In those sultry August and September days the foreign press called the Germans barbarians and cited Nietzsche, Treitschke, and Bernhardi as the intellectual instigators of the war. If you mix all three together and sift out all that is clever or intellectually fine, the remainder will be the stuff of which Count Reventlow is made. A bull-headed man whom life had thrown around recklessly; a man of no preconceived ideas, politically frivolous, an unconstrained and unrestrained being who appeals to instinct more than reason — put such a man in a responsible position and you may see for yourself whither it must lead.

XXIV

GEORG MICHAELIS

I open my political diary at the date, March 7, 1917. A little sensation in the House of Representatives. The new Prussian Food Commissioner, a tiny dried-up man, with a face like a parrot, introduced himself to the Reichstag in a somewhat unusual manner. Venus sprung from the sea foam, Michaelis from the dust of legal documents. This little fellow dived up all of a sudden from behind the speaker's desk, and began playing Napoleon. Fearfully he swashed the air with the sword of his spirit. "The office laid upon me is born of the heavy troubles inflicted upon us." He then unrolled the problem of who is to blame, slashed right and left, flayed the Junkers and agrarians for feeding their live stock instead of delivering the grain to the magistrate. The eyes of the Conservatives opened wider and wider. When he heard the grumbling and growling going on beneath him he played his last trump: "Who is to gainsay me! I would like to know who will succeed in hindering me if I do my duty in this point!" Oi, oi, they thought, this little man slashes right well with his insufficient strength and weak voice. Comedy or tragedy? But he continues: "I will take over no office that is like a sword without sharpness, nor will I keep a position which is apt to dull my own sword. I will fight on with the help of Him who watches over the German people." There was nothing lacking but, "Here I am, Lord. I could not do otherwise, God help me, Amen."

On the way home I spoke with several gentlemen of the Left who had been impressed by the tiny man with the Bible and the catechism on the end of his tongue. "He's a fine little fellow, all the same," said one. "He got the National Granary Department in working order, put our bread supply on a firm footing, and he is not afraid to tell the Conservatives what he thinks."

"Do you know more about him?"

"A little. He comes from a large Silesian family. His father was district judge. He is the third of seven children. Georg himself has six. His oldest, a mere lad, fell in the war. For a time Michaelis was director of the school and church department of the Arnsberg Government. Later he went to Breslau as Councillor of the Präsidium; did all he could to relieve the misery at the time of the flood along the Oder in 1903. Then he entered the Ministry of Finance, became under-secretary, and during the war worked at the head of the grain department. He spent four years teaching in Tokio at the school of German law and political science. He is sixty years old, and that is about all I know about him."

March 27, 1917. To-day I received a hasty invitation to a conference with Dr. Georg Michaelis in the Ministry of Finance. I went this afternoon. The house on Kupfergraben could stand a little paint. It is nothing but angular little office rooms. It has a military atmosphere and needs nothing but a sentry-box outside and a corporal within. A long corridor leads to a small conference room where there is a long, green table and an official corona. The Commissioner arrived, everybody bowed. He seated himself, pulled out a gold watch, opened it and laid it on the desk in front of him. Then he began to speak dryly, slowly, and in a business-like manner. Once he allowed his confidence in Hindenburg and Ludendorff to peep through. As we went down the street we agreed: "A sort of upper Councillor who would like to play Caesar."

July 13, 1917. The Chancellor crisis is in full swing. Bethmann-Hollweg is not to be held back since the "Stein" (stone) has been removed from his path. The highest military authorities, the leading Conservatives, the most influential Junkers, could not shake the Kaiser's faith in him. "Stein or me." "To be or not to be," was now the war-cry, and Bethmann fell. Many a name was mentioned as his successor; just for a joke I will tell you that Michaelis' name was also mentioned.

GEORG MICHAELIS

We laughed about it in our wine-room, but a politician said we should see.

July 14, 1917. It came like a bomb: Michaelis — Chancellor! No one was even asked. Not a soul knew it beforehand. Like a thunderbolt it fell out of a clear sky. A nice kettle of fish for Germany! Even the Kaiser didn't know him. He had been recommended to the Empress as especially pious. And just think of what he had accomplished! He had apportioned our daily bread for three years; why should he not be able to treat the people well who had grown up on his bread? Someone from the Chancellery told me that when he telephoned the news to his wife she merely said, "You're crazy!" Whether or not he echoed a pious Amen to this I do not know. The press did not greet him so badly. The *Tägliche Rundschau* proudly called him "Our Chancellor," for they had recommended him. Only the Left wing grumbled because he had been foisted upon them in this manner.

July 18, 1917. He is a funny bird, this Michaelis. He confesses he has not had any more political experience than the average politician. As head of the Chancelry he appoints a certain director of the Fat Department, a Landrat von Graevenitz. Butter, oil, and wagon grease spread themselves around in Bismarck's rooms.

July 19, 1917. Michaelis makes his great speech in the Reichstag after the parliamentary, ministerial, and military conference in Herr Helfferich's garden is ended. He wanted to acknowledge his desire for a peace without annexation or compensation. Wanted to — but all at once in the middle of his peroration he added, half-audibly, this little sentence: "These aims can be accomplished within the compass of the resolutions — as I understand them."

July 20, 1917. We didn't see the little back door that Michaelis — his eyes turned toward Heaven — suddenly opened. Now with the printed speech before us, and the words, "as I understand them," staring us in the face, we began to scent trouble. In a trice he had discredited the Government at home and abroad. One does not get very far with such dishonorable methods.

July 30, 1917. At last it is possible to see what effect his Reichstag speech made on the outer world. A catastrophe! They mistrust Germany altogether. "German faith, German wine, German song." Herr Michaelis gambled away our faith, as a Christian teetotaler or better, as a friend of moderation, he despises German wine, and as for song, he knows only the choral book.

August 6, 1917. It is amusing to see how Herr Michaelis enjoys his revenge. All the gentlemen who were his superiors or who had made him uncomfortable in one way or another were now, one after another strangled with the silken string, "canned" in other words. His chief but yesterday, Dr. Lentze, was the first to go. Herr Batocki, president of the Food Commission, was sent to Königsberg, although he had hoped to be sent only as far as Leipzigerplatz. It was not a pleasant aspect.

August 20, 1917. To-day the chief of the Chancelry plunged excitedly toward the gentlemen of the press and begged them for God's sake not to mention what had happened. It was a misunderstanding, a mistake — we all knew the Michaelis melody. He had gone back on the aims of the commission and announced casually that he had never approved of their purposes. This time the Left tripped him up and he was summoned to a painful examination; he stammered a few embarrassed words and had to apologize to the Reichstag. They said he will only last until holiday time.

September 4, 1917. It wasn't a bad idea of Michaelis' to call in the council of seven to discuss the answer to the Pope's note. The Reichstag was politically satisfied.

September 6, 1917. Michaelis has performed the most unbelievable trick. He spoke of a mutiny which had been discovered and put down, accusing the Independent Socialists of taking part in the complot. There was tremendous excitement. The enemy could laugh and triumph once more. Will he stay at his post any longer?

LEADERS OF YESTERDAY AND TO-DAY

October 10, 1917. He tried to make a goat of Herr von Capelle, father of the childish attack on the Left. But it didn't work this time. It was a test of strength, he had to go.

October 11, 1917. The Reichstag sent a deputation to convince him how very badly the nation did not need him. He became hard of hearing.

October 12, 1917. He still considered himself indispensable. At least he would have liked to retain the leadership of the Prussian ministry. Count Hertling refused — either everything or nothing.

November 2, 1917. Michaelis submitted, thank God.

July 14, 1918. Herr Michaelis has been president in Stettin for a long time. Every morning he says his prayers and feels himself quite happy as the subordinate of those he once elevated. The "last shall be first and the first shall be last"— he has had a taste of both. Like the fairy tale of Haroun-al Raschid, who put a beggar on the throne for a day, this joke cost Germany two years of war and hundreds of thousands of victims. The oriental fairy tale was less expensive.

August 30, 1918. In his election speech Conrad Haussmann spoke the right word: "I accuse the former Imperial Chancellor, Michaelis, with not having followed the policy laid down by Prince Max von Baden — he sowed the seeds of mistrust against us, and doubt as to our intentions."

XXV

GUSTAV STRESEMANN

As Ernst Basserman, head of the National Liberal party, lay upon his sick bed watching the Reaper slowly drawing nigh, three pretenders to his throne were making ready to step into his boots: Friedberg, Schiffer, and Stresemann. Each one felt himself a secret crown prince. But Fate was cunning; before there was time for a rivalry to develop, she found a different post for all three. Friedberg, former professor of political science, was appointed to the vice-presidency of the Ministry by Count Hertling; Schiffer received an honorable post in the treasury; and Stresemann was chosen by the party as chairman of the Reichstag faction — Bassermann's old place. Bassermann was at heart a liberal man, but hundreds of compromises with the conservatives and the dictation of big industrialists had made him politically and bodily irritable. The national idealistic professors, Gneist and Sybel, once set the pace for the party; under Bassermann it passed through the agrarian-capitalistic crisis. When one could go no further toward the Right,— when, as Dernburg said, one bumped against the wall,— he rooted out the agrarian sore and turned his eyes toward the Left. The capitalists whose money helped to keep the treasury full, began to raise their voices in warning to their unfaithful servant. Frictions arose. Under the leadership of Mr. Fuhrmann, the old National Liberal national organization revived, and a noisy party battle ensued. Young Liberals, old Liberals, and the Basserman National Liberal guard swung their swords against one another and the battle raged in the columns of the press. Only the outbreak of war put an end to this ruinous strife for awhile. But it broke out again when the capitalists, at first secretly, then openly, manifested their annexationist aims; when they fought against every political change in Prussian Germany; when they drew one paper after the other into their services, especially the *Berliner Neuesten Nachrichten* and the *Deutscher Kurier;* and lastly when their relations to the Alldeutschen League grew warmer and warmer. This was the blow that killed Bassermann. Gustav Stresemann, who grew up in industrial circles either as general secretary or syndikus, took over the leadership of the party.

Did the big industrialists come off victors? Whoever judges so superficially does not know the psychology of the National Liberal party. In the breast of every National Liberalist live two, three, and sometimes four souls. Sometimes there is a transmigration of these souls. At bottom everyone is national. Many a compromise is covered by this uncertain and much meaning word. Secondly, the National Liberal is liberal. At least that is what the program says. But there is many a hitch in the practice of this sentiment. Richthofen, Riesser, Böhme, Junck, Schönaich-Carolath are really liberal and not mere pretenders. But Fuhrmann, Hirsch, and consorts — what have they to do with liberalism? If one travels in the provinces one will find that the national and liberal men are the teachers, district judges, and small industrialists. Beyond this border line begin economic interests which seek to influence the party. Dr. Stresemann is the perfect type of factory representative, a general secretary, of which the National Liberal party has more than any other. But he is only a stepmother to really large industries. He was born in Berlin forty years ago, studied political science and history in Berlin and Leipzig and began a technical career at the age of twenty-three. He began as assistant in the German Chocolate Manufacturers' Union. A year later he helped to found the Saxon Manufacturers' Union and became their recorder without giving up his other post. Other corporations soon sought his services and his income increased accordingly. As wholesale recorder he possessed some little influence. In the intervals he wrote on the most impossible subjects: shops, bottled beer trade, landworkers' organization, and factory doings. As a side issue he published the *Sächsische Industrie*. Always working and striving, his strong constitution made it possible for him to accomplish a full day's work with ease. He spoke as he wrote, indefatigably. Naturally he wished to enter the Reichstag. In 1907 he was sent to the Reichstag from Annaberg. Skilled in business, and with far-reaching personal relations, he was soon respected in the faction, although he did not speak all too frequently at first. But he spoke often and willingly to public gatherings — liked to speak on public occasions such as national holidays and Bismarck celebrations. He spoke in a strong voice with a slight, provincial accent; people liked to listen to him. He seemed to have acquired a National Liberal spirit with his mother's milk.

And yet this was not the case. When quite a young man he had been very socialistic. Seventeen years ago he went to Frankfurt-am-Main as a delegate of Dresden's National Socialists. It was here that Friedrich Naumann condemned the Richter and Bassermann type of liberalism. "If you put all the National Liberal representatives together from Paasche to Bassermann," Naumann said, "and try to find one constructive economic idea among them, you will find nothing but chaos." Among those who applauded enthusiastically was Dr. Stresemann. When the Hamburg group discussed passing a resolution against alcoholism he told them he was convinced laws would serve no purpose. "If we put war against alcoholism on our program," he said, "then we shall have to proclaim a war for vegetarianism." The broad-shouldered man shuddered at such a step — he liked his food.

Another moment from these party days where we find Brentano, Sohm, Damaschke, and Weinhausen together, Stresemann, who now wrote for the *Tägliche Rundschau,* brought a choleric accusation against this paper: "The National Socialist party protest against the hateful and unjust personal attacks against their leaders, which the *Tägliche Rundschau* prints in her columns. We expect a feeling of honor to prevent our comrades from having anything to do with such a paper."

That was seventeen years ago. Since then he had forgotten and forgiven. The next step was Young Liberalism. He lost in the next election in 1912, and also the one after that. Then he gave up the Saxon-Thuringia districts and went over to Hanover, the home of National Liberalism, where he won. His place in the Reichstag was still warm, and as Herr Bassermann retired more and more on account of ill-health, he soon became the second ornament on the list of speakers until he finally became leader of the faction. His paper was the *Deutsche Stimmen,* the leading National Liberal weekly. He wrote the leading editorial, the political review, which he handled delicately, signing his articles with a triangle.

Dr. Stresemann is not original; he is not prominent in the sense of Richter, Bennigsen, Windhorst or Bebel, but he is clever, skillful and active — virtues which the party needed most at that time. Large ideas would have probably been the end of the party, which was not very steady. The battle for predominance went on. Would he meet this dragon with a flaming sword? Sometimes it seemed so. During the war he made arrangements for political changes in the party, declared equal suffrage to be absolutely necessary in Prussia, and was not against a parliamentary system.

On the other hand, he helped to bring about Bethmann-Hollweg's fall, smoothed the way for such a man as Michaelis, and at every opportunity preached a peace of might with annexations and compensation. In order not to lose his connections with the Left entirely, he took part in the conference of the majority, but only for a short time. The continual cry of the annexationists and the capitalists scared him, and the strike movement in January, 1918, gave him the excuse for breaking off his relations with the Social Democrats. He was glad to be out of it, to be rid of all responsibility, and waited for the miracle which would make the National Liberal policy synonymous with a governmental policy. But it happened otherwise. The great change came, Count

GUSTAV STRESEMANN

Hertling fell, Prince Max von Baden took his place, and the parliamentary system came over night. The leaders of the majority took over the Government. Under Stresemann's leadership the party held sittings almost every morning and afternoon in the days of September and October, 1918. Why? They were discussing the "situation." In reality they were waiting for the Government and the majority to take pity on them and invite them to take part in the program. Stresemann was baptized the "political tree frog" in those days because he jumped whichever way the wind blew, thereby happily losing his contact on all sides. The majority parties were hard of hearing; democracy did not wish to burden itself with such slippery fish as the Stresemann outfit. Finally, Herr von Payer, the Vice-Chancellor, uttered the wish that the National Liberals might be allowed to participate. "But," he said, "the National Liberals must bend their necks under the yoke of our program. The National Liberalists and Herr Stresemann did so. They scraped and kotowed. In one hour the savage annexationists became the most convinced adherents of a peace without annexation, joyful champions of the Reichstag peace resolutions of July 19, 1917, true friends of the League of Nations idea. Thank God, Herr Stresemann had found his bearings once more. The turning point must come soon.

Things went on in this fashion for about six weeks;

then came the revolution that washed them all overboard. The National Liberal party went to pieces. The newly-arisen German Democratic party threatened to swallow them all. They politely rejected such compromised, political turncoats as Herr Stresemann and company. Stresemann, full of injured vanity, gathered up the last remnants of the National Liberal party, plastered them together, and anointed the whole of the new German People's party. He had *someone* behind him again, if it were only capitalists and old National Liberalists. For a change he stood first on one foot and then on the other, in order not to lose his connections.

XXVI

LOTHAR PERSIUS

"I do not understand the man! Grown gray in the service as sea captain, and now — pacifist!"

"Yes, captain, but have you ever tried to understand the psychology of this man? Of course, those who have nothing to do but command are not in the habit of paying much attention to psychology. That is why officers and school directors are such poor psychologists."

"Is that so! I dispute that seriously. We who have to deal with people from every station in life get a deep look into the souls of mankind every day. You see, Persius is angered and embittered because he received the blue envelope just before he should have become Rear Admiral. That is my psychological analysis. No need for subtleties where everything is as plain as the nose on your face."

"You simplify the matter greatly, captain. You command and I have but to obey. But as I am not your subordinate I reserve the right to contradict you."

Let us calmly and coolly dissect this man.

He comes from an old and very respected family to whom Prussian tradition is a sort of Kultur-conservatism, bourgeois, Potsdam atmosphere. A number of our officers and officials have come from this family.

His grandfather was a royal architect and curator of artistic monuments. The oldest of his four sons became acting Privy Councillor with the title of Excellence, and was president of the Supreme Court of Berlin for twenty-six years. For a time he was member of the Reichstag. Fundamentally a thoroughly conservative man but liberal in his manners. He did not entrench himself behind documents as behind a Chinese wall, and he had understanding for all that was human and a weakness for art. The knowledge gained in a court of law peeped through now and then. For instance, it was he who permitted Gerhard Hauptmann's *Weavers* to be performed although those up above wrinkled their brows in disapproval.

This was Lothar Persius' father. Lothar inherited similar traits from his mother. She was a von Zander, daughter of a Geheimrat and niece of the Chancellor von Zander. Wherever you look you see officers and officials in her family. Is it any wonder that Lothar looks the typical, clean-cut Prussian officer? In spite of his fifty-five years he is still sinewy and supple.

When he left the Friedrich-Wilhelm gymnasium in Berlin, he felt a call to the navy. " You can become a cavalry officer if you do not care to study any more, but don't go to sea," pleaded his mother. In those days honorable mothers and fathers had the idea that only prodigal sons went to sea.

But he got his way. He came into the world at the right moment, just as Germany stretched out her arms to grasp a few colonies. As naval cadet, he sailed around the world on the *Elizabeth,* and witnessed the founding of the colonies in Africa, New Guinea, and Polynesia. As officer, he sailed his ship in the Mediterranean, to North and South America, and witnessed the taking of Manila during the Spanish war. At the beginning of this century he was first officer and commander of the cruisers *Hansa* and *Seeadler* in East Asia for years.

Up to this time the course of his life ran smoothly and pleasantly. Fate seemed only to show her sunny side. When he had to do battle it was only on the field of sports. How he could trim his sails! How his yacht flew over the water like a sea-gull, bringing him one trophy after the other: silver and gold cups, writing sets, and so on! He was frequently with Prince Heinrich and His Majesty. The Kaiser once smiled pleasantly when Persius said: "Married officers are only half-fighters. They are always thinking of wife and children which makes them over-careful."

The first conflict came in East Asia. After a few literary flights on the sport subjects, Persius began to criticize with his pen. As an officer he wrote under a pseudonym. The *Ostasiatische Lloyd* published several of his severely critical articles on the military colonization methods in Kiaochow. The author became known and there was a stir up above. Once more he made himself objectionable. His superior officers asked him to make a report demanding more table money for officers stationed in foreign countries. Persius, however, was of another opinion. " Table money is already more than sufficient," he wrote, supporting this statement by statistics from his own carefully kept accounts.

He was finally sent to Kiel as director of the ammunition depots in Dietrichsdorf by Kiel. His naval career was nearing its end. In October, 1908, he was retired and went to live in Berlin. An energetic man with wholly unused powers, released from the narrow confines of military life, he sought new goals and new aims in life. His sphere of interest was not small; yachting, belles-lettres, music, art, naval technic, and politics. The papers gladly opened their columns to this man who had much specialized knowledge and a clever pen.

In the *Jahrbücher für Armee und Marine* he investigated Herr von Tirpitz's accomplishments in the way of ship-building, and came to no favorable conclusion. This happened during his stay in Kiel and soon had its consequences. Now that he was free, and free also from party prejudices, he began to write for the *Tägliche Rundschau,* the *Berliner Neuesten Nachrichten, Deutsche Zeitung,* and the red *Tag.*

In all his articles he continually pointed out Tirpitz's mistaken naval policy. Hermes, former editor-in-chief of the *Kreuzzeitung,* begged him to work for his paper and help stem the disastrous tide of Tirpitz's folly, until subscribers and supporters of Tirpitz's policy compelled him to seek another editor for the naval column. For a time Persius wrote the naval review for the red *Tag.* In 1912 the *Berliner Tageblatt* offered him the proper sounding board for his much respected naval criticism.

Persius belonged to the Navy Verein for a few years at the time when General Keim was storming against Tirpitz. Keim was for larger guns, more U-boats,— in short, a more modern equipment of the navy. After the shock of Keim's resignation, when Admirals von Koester and Weber took over the Verein, it soon became manifest they were only tools of the National Naval Department. The coöperation of a man like Persius was no longer possible, and he slowly withdrew from these circles.

It was not entirely differences of opinion in regard to the fleet that forced him to resign; he began to see the evil effects of the noisy naval propaganda. He who knew England and the English so well, saw that this agitation would sooner or later lead to war with that country. So he became pacifist because he foresaw the horrors that would be inflicted upon humanity if there were not some steps taken toward a compromise. He welcomed the English proposition for a "Naval Year" and fought against the building of battleships instead of submarines, hoping to avoid rivalry in this way. In 1912 he wrote: *U-boat an die Front!* which attracted attention in all circles. Almost everything he prophesied here has come to pass. After that he became more and more pacific. He was coworker on the *Friedenswarte,* and published at the instigation of Andrew Carnegie a book on the possibility of doing away with armament rivalry. His numerous articles in the *Berliner Tageblatt* enjoyed especial attention and red lead-penciling in the censor room of the Naval Department.

"Good gracious, aren't you through with Persius' biography yet?"

"Almost, Captain. We are coming to the end. Are you still convinced that Captain Persius took to the pen merely because he was angry at being retired? The fact is he began to write while still an active officer. And the war has proved that he was right in suggesting the building of submarines, in contrast to Tirpitz, who would hear nothing of those 'horrible U-boats' at first. Afterwards when he was forced to accept this policy, he posed as the U-boat hero. He who follows a naval policy so unswervingly and consecutively as Persius has done, is surely actuated by more than a personal grudge."

"But you owe me an answer to one question, and that is: How is he to be politically defined?"

"That is not easy to say. He belongs among those who feel aristocratic, but who think democratically, who must think this way because their reason compels them to. No doubt this is the cause of inner conflicts, but the mental aristocrat conquers because uncontrollable and uncertain emotions are subordinate to the better insight of reason."

"One thing more: foreign countries suck poison from his articles."

"How so? Merely because the English and French press value his criticisms?"

"Surely, that is why"—

"That is why one should not express one's opinion? There are other men in leading positions who think as you do, Captain. It was representative Gothein who said on the 15th of June of this year: 'As the representative of the Naval Department has already said, Persius' articles must be scrutinized narrowly because he is praised in England for his technical knowledge. For this very reason his articles are extremely dangerous.'"

"I think we shall have to break off. You cannot shake my opinion of Captain Persius and besides that, here we are in Potsdam and I have to get to my barracks. Adieu . . ."

XXVII

FRIEDRICH VON PAYER

On the third floor of the Reichstag building they are getting a room ready for a meeting of the Progressive People's party; long rows of tables end against a table standing parallel to the window. From this window one can look down upon Königsplatz. Large paintings decorate the walls, pictures from German history. Among them is Wilhelm the First's triumphal entry of 1870 — the Kaiser on horseback, passing between French flags lowered almost to the dust. We know that this picture was meant for another room — for the assembly room — but it caused so much displeasure on the other side of the Vosges that it was relegated to this room, where no one but members was allowed to enter.

A little party meeting was to take place behind closed doors. Here where so many secret things had been confided to the representatives, where once Bethmann-Hollweg announced an unrestricted submarine warfare, Herr von Payer, a Württemberg Excellence, discussed the political situation. He was the first war Chancellor. A large manuscript was spread out in front of him;

FRIEDRICH VON PAYER

near him, wearing horn spectacles, sat a Herr Funck from Frankfurt am Main, chairman of the Central committee. Sitting in a row were: Dr. Otto Weimer, once Eugen Richter's pupil, now first tenor of the party (Wagner rôles — Tannhäuser, Siegfried, Tristan); then Rector Julius Kopsch, bass buffo in progressive concert ensemble, the man who always sought to disarm the enemy in his own camp with honeyed pathos; Dr. Friedrich Naumann, lyrical tenor, political moral trumpeter from Säckingen; Dr. Pachnicke, ingenue, with the shy and tender upward glance; Mr. Hoff, the country maiden, with chubby, brown cheeks; Georg Gothein, the fiery lover; Bank Director Mommsen, the elderly, village heroine; Dr. Struve, the witty aperçu; Dr. Müller-Meiningen, the jack-in-the-box with "a gift of gab"; Professor Quidde, the pacifist circuit-rider, and a lot more. One hundred and fifty men, representatives and delegates from every nook and cranny of the kingdom,— the journalists.

Herr von Payer did not carry the audience with him, but his Swabian dialect lent a comfortable air to his words. His head was slightly bent forward; in spite of his seventy years the hair was all there. There was not a single white thread in those black locks. A beard rested upon his bosom, and out of two small caverns gleamed two little, dark-brown eyes.

He had the confidence of the whole party; a long,

democratic past justified it. He worked side by side with Rickert, Richter, Sonnemann, and all the rest who are now lying in their graves — with Windhorst, Grillenberger, Bebel, Singer, and the old Liebknecht, against Bismarck's law-making.

At twenty-six years of age he was candidate for the Reichstag from Tübingen, where his father was beadle of the university. He was not elected but went to Stuttgart and settled down as a lawyer. Later he was elected to the Württemberger Iandtag, became president, was decorated by the King, knighted, and received the title of Excellence. He was always the most popular person in Swabia, was our Payer; and always the smooth and clear-cut democrat.

His political accomplishments are not to be despised. It was partly his work that the National Liberals and independent organizations were united under the name of the new Progressive People's party. He became leader of this new faction in the Reichstag, and if Herr Weimer had not lifted up his sonorous voice he would have been the party mouthpiece.

Two or three times his friends shook their heads; how could even such a dyed-in-the-wool democrat take part in Bülow's block swindle? It was like mixing fire and water. How was it possible in this joyless epoch for liberalism — for Herr von Payer — ostentatiously to approve of the foreign language paragraph, which bore all the earmarks of an exceptional law? Herr von Payer made this sacrifice with a heavy heart in order to keep the block together and to insure some progress for the law.

Like Bethmann-Hollweg, who discarded his conservatism more and more during the war as he gained a deeper insight into its causes, so von Payer found a Swiss guard in the Progressive People's party who watched over his comings and goings. Herr von Payer was half mockingly, half respectfully, called the Pillar of Wilhelmstrasse. Together with Herr Spahn, he was the party diplomat, the real pacifier when the waves on the Left threatened to rise. And yet he was unable to prevent Bethman-Hollweg's fall. Everybody deserted the Chancellor in his hour of need, although at midnight before his resignation he succeeded in wringing equal suffrage for Prussia from the Kaiser. The National Liberals put the knife in his back, and the Crown Prince, not the Kaiser, called on the party leaders for their opinion in regard to Bethmann-Hollweg. They said their say to a wholly political, irresponsible personage — Westarp, Stresemann, Spahn, Payer, and David. The first two merely said he was a crawfish. (A year later in 1918, Dr. Stresemann, the political tree-frog, together with the whole National Liberal faction, were marching with drum and trumpet under the "crawfish.") Herr Spahn, his little legs trembling, said they did not like to lose the Chancellor, no, no, they did not like to, and Herr David pulled a sour face at the name and at the behest of social democracy. Only the valiant Swabian manfully supported the Chancellor. His Royal Highness, however, had already made up his mind, lit a cigarette and was royally calm. Had not the gentlemen representatives themselves unanimously dropped this disgusting, three-quarter social democrat pusher? And did not the philosophy of might teach: always kick a fellow when he is down?

From this day German parliamentarism was a confirmed fact. The Left and the Center united, forming an interfactional commission. Fifty years after the foundation of the North German Bund, the Reichstag gradually began to feel itself on equal terms with the Bundesrat and the Government. Herr von Payer was chairman of this commission which had no power according to law, but which nevertheless represented a mighty political force. Its first test of strength was against Michaelis; they were not inclined to work any longer with this Imperial Chancellor. In spite of a struggle he had to go. Count Hertling was the first to act as a politician in a parliamentary governed state. He assured himself of the confidence of the majority and after a program was agreed upon he called von Payer into the cabinet as Vice-Chancellor. Payer accepted this position, moved into a modest little office in the

FRIEDRICH VON PAYER

Department of the Interior, and looked about for a stenographer and a typewriting machine — a small beginning. He waited for work and it soon came.

In the general strike of 1918 he played the rôle of arbitrator, not without success; on the 25th of February he made his maiden speech as Vice-Chancellor, not from the Government table but from the speaker's platform, in order to make a show as parliament minister. He came into conflict with the conservatives because he supported equal suffrage and condemned their wild, political agitation during the past strike. "Our enemies have their choice of weapons," he resumed. "They may use the arrows either of the Right or of the Left wing against us." This had an explosive effect. The conservatives went wild over the comparison. In their excitement some sprung from their seats; Payer remained calm while listening to such remarks as: "Is this a party gathering?" "So that's the great statesman!" "Unheard of!" etc. The president tried to call the house to order, but his wildly swinging bell had no effect whatever. Herr von Payer had just made a confession of democratic faith.

He repeated this when making his Stuttgart speech in which he laid down the war aims of Germany. He spoke openly and freely for a democratic peace, declared himself ready to give up Belgium, to renounce all annexations or compensations, and pointed out the necessity of an international court, a league of nations, and universal disarmament. Only in the Eastern problem did he take an opposite stand. He wished to exclude this question from the peace discussion altogether.

Again the conservatives and Alldeutschers boiled over; there was a racket without equal in the press. The *Tägliche Rundschau,* foaming with rage, accused him of taking Goethe's saying for a motto: "One always denies and denies with justice that nobility can never learn anything." Another Pan-German organ said pointedly that the name Payer could mean nothing but the French word "payer," therefore he must have originally come from France and it was no wonder.

Herr von Payer merely smiled with the same calmness he displayed in rejecting the Chancellorship which was offered him when Count Hertling retired. He only wished to be a pioneer of the new epoch. Then came the revolution and washed him away on its waves. Finally the new election carried him into the National Assembly, where, for a while, he played the part of a leader of the Democratic faction.

XXVIII

KUNO GRAF VON WESTARP

On the 15th of May, 1879, Eugen Richter characterized Bismarck's political methods in a very few words. The question of power, he said, was always the chief problem of the Chancellor. "In foreign affairs it was his clever handling of this question, of the relations of power, that won him the most success. His great mistake was that he transferred this method of action to home politics in an unjust manner . . . The Chancellor brings the whole power of state to bear against a mere party, thereby arousing the people. Later he follows up this action as if it concerned a question of power which can only be disposed of by a diplomatic compromise." These words were spoken at a turning point in young Germany's political life. For the first time Bismarck began to doubt the success of a clashing Kultur war. He needed the Center's support for his new protective tariff and economic schemes. At least a part of the National Liberals seemed about to desert him. His whole volcanic hatred was now directed against social democracy which he held responsible for the attentat against his royal masters. A new era of

LEADERS OF YESTERDAY AND TO-DAY

exceptional law-making began. After the Berlin Congress he lost favor with Russia and adopted a defensive policy with Austria-Hungary. This and the annexation of Alsace-Lorraine were the seeds of the present world war. The theory of power, in spite of Nietzsche's hoarse enthusiasm, did not seem entirely unquestionable to the succeeding generations. If one wishes to give this great struggle of nations an ethical meaning it is the thought that through blood and iron alone will this idea of power be forever done away with, at least as far as international politics are concerned.

Kuno Graf von Westarp does not subscribe to this theory; he is a disciple of the theory of might through and through,— a fanatic opponent of social democracy. This East Elbian Junker is an adept of Otto von Bismarck. In 1918 Westarp was playing a leading rôle in parliament although he had only been a member for ten years. After Herr von Naumann's death, von Heydebrand became chief of the conservative faction, but after transferring his main activity to the threatened Prussian three-class Landtag, Westarp became the almost undisputed leader of this faction. Here he was the big gun of the party, and every Sunday in the *Kreuzzeitung* he gave a carefully composed recapitulation of conservative doings for the week. A small cross resembling the iron one was his literary sign. He wrote as he spoke: sharp, cutting, clear, and calm, without developing any large or surprising ideas. He spoke from a wholly one-sided, almost scholastic-conservative point of view. There was no understanding or forgiving, no penetration into the psychology of the other party; there was but an unswerving adherence to one's own, to the historical, and an absolute rejection of all that did not fit into his scheme. He was a perfect example of the uncompromising; one froze in this political rigidity, in this iron consequence; one could almost see him writing with folded arms (if you allow me this bold comparison) just as he sat when Bethmann-Hollweg was talking.

He was the exact opposite of Herr Heydebrand, who played with things pleasantly and smoothly, often bubbling over with wit. Westarp was hard and cold, puritanic; he stood there like a public moralist to whom politics was something frozenly objective. In reality they were subjective, unfathomable, concealing in themselves thousandfold contrasts. All sorts of things played a part: birth, social milieu, education, brain capacity, emotional life, practical experience, etc. Westarp liked to examine everybody politically; would have liked to play the rôle of political confessor to the Government. Because things have taken another course, because Bethmann-Hollweg turned a cold shoulder to the conservatives, because Count Hertling, although maintaining the outward form, was even further from the conservative line and left them entirely out of the new People's Government, Westarp's weekly articles have taken on a somewhat crabbed and bitter tone — something like that of a police commissioner too early pensioned.

This is not a bad comparison as Westarp has had a great deal to do with the police. His father was head forester. He died when Kuno was but four years of age. Westarp attended the Potsdam gymnasium, attended three or four universities, studied law, and took up the usual Government career. Fate kept him in the Ostmark. He became assistant Landrat, the Landrat in the idyllic district of Bomst. After a short period elsewhere he was called to the Department of the Interior, where his upward climb soon began. In April, 1905, he was appointed police director of Schöneberg, later becoming president of police, and in another five years was justice of the Supreme Court. He still holds this office and also that of lieutenant of the militia. He is fifty-six years old. The district where he was once Landrat sent him to the Reichstag. He had to battle against a Center man in 1908. The prospects were not particularly favorable. He made a profession of anti-Semitism and pulled through on the Jewish vote. In 1912 his position was more favorable for the Conservatives presented a united front to the Poles, and

KUNO GRAF VON WESTARP

Westarp laid out his opponent flat. After that he governed rigidly within the boundaries of conservatism — even deigning to spread a little propaganda now and then among the masses.

Count Westarp is one of those who cannot forget — he is like an uncanny, party, political-register, like a walking bureau of acts in which the sins of the others are carefully filed away. His articles are valuable material for the conservative propaganda; he unconsciously plays the rôle of political coach.

Indefatigably industrious, he is always Johnny-on-the-spot in the Reichstag. He sits on his flap seat under the Chancellor's place ever ready to spring up with a protest on his lips. A secret Cromwell (just the other way about) ready to stake his life for his king — ready to lead a Puritan squadron to free his monarch from the snares of anti-king Demos. This is the way it looks in a romance. In reality he represents a small clique — a Junker caste — who have lost almost all but the name.

Count Kuno is one of those whose task it is to cover the retreat of the Junkers. He has found his place in the new conservative firm, the German National People's party, even if he was not a candidate for a seat in the National Assembly on account of being a "compromised personage."

XXIX

HUGO HAASE

In the Reichstag Hugo Haase sat on the left by the wall; I still see him abruptly barking his remonstrances in broad, somewhat ordinary, East Prussian dialect. It sounded like a voice coming up from the deepest depths, a rasping bass from a great hollow cask booming, " Crucify him! " It was a great contrast to the high falsetto of the step-softly's and compromisers in the Parliament. When Haase gave the signal his comrades gave tongue in quick succession — Dittman, Herzfeld, Stadthagen, Cohn, Wurm, down to Liebknecht and Rühle, until the noise swelled to a roaring chorus. This storm of applause or disapproval which always broke forth on the dot, swelling from muttering thunder to a raging tornado, was never carried out with the same success by anyone else but the Haase group which formed only about one twentieth of the whole House. I remember distinctly how Dittmann's attack against the prison disgrace succeeded by this clever move — he even carried the Center and the National-Liberals with him. But they were much worse among themselves. When Haase and his people quarreled with

HUGO HAASE

the majority Social Democrats, it looked as if they would spring at each other's throats every minute — Haase, the wild revolutionist, leading the pack.

Is he really so revolutionary? Appearances deceive. Perhaps he is only a fanatic for truth, one who honestly takes the consequences of his belief. He is a small, unpretending little man, shy and repressed, with a yellow, wrinkled face and thin, drooping mustache, small, nervous gray eyes under tired, half-closed lids. His bent back looks like a youth at hard labor.

God knows his youth was joyless enough. Do you know the existence of a Jewish small trader in a little town on the borders of East Germany? Well-fed, comfortable citizens, feudal Junkers from the country as guests, bored poker-playing, cavalry officers — that was and still is the milieu. And the little parasitic Jew in their midst, whose services are so often required. He was born in 1863, near Albenstein before it had a railway station or became the seat of a commanding general. He attended the Gymnasium of Rastenburg and later studied law at the University of Königsberg.

It was a tedious road to climb but he trod the thorny path alone. Could he take up a Government career? Ridiculous! After passing his examinations he became a lawyer. He was clear, logical, and possessed a store of hard-earned knowledge; above all, he was a man who retained a sympathetic heart in spite of life's bitterness. He lusted not after gold or social position, but remained at the bottom helping the poor. He became the proletariat's lawyer in Königsberg and his practice grew from day to day. Often he was not paid and many a time he reached into his own pocket to help a needy client. The confidence of the people soon sent him to the Königsberg city council; in 1897 to the Reichstag, where he quickly won the liking of the party patriarch, Bebel.

His radicalism made an impression. He knew how to win his comrades on party days, for he was not like Ledebour, who opposed for the mere sake of opposition. He had higher things in view. There was always understanding for practical questions or tactics if they did not affect his fundamental principles. Only against revisionism he fought with fire and sword. This was a disease which must be stamped out. He settled the score with Kurt Eisner, the brilliant author of the *Vorwärts* leading articles, and placed Hildebrand, the social-imperial, colonial politician, before a court of inquisition. In the meantime he had become chairman of the party. Out of love for the ideals of socialism he gave up a lucrative law practice and lived upon the meager sum of 3600 marks, his salary as head of the party. Singer, his predecessor, was of a genial, open nature, a personified Bonhomie. Haase was industrious, taciturn, unapproachable, with no particular friends.

HUGO HAASE

Then came the war. The Socialistic Internationale was to stand its first trial by fire. On the evening before the decision Haase chased his people out on the streets to demonstrate for peace. I witnessed the battalion of workers as they marched through the streets of Leipzig. But the Marseillaise sounded flat and dull. Too soon Haase had let his comrades on the other side know that German social democracy would try to hinder the war. They had depended upon this and were disappointed. The 4th of August saw German social democracy, with Haase, almost to a man behind the Government. Things went on this way for a while. War credit was voted for, but, under the covers, opposition within the party was gradually beginning to stir. At the beginning of April, 1915, a socialistic minority sent a peace manifest to all foreign countries. An announcement from Hugo Haase, Eduard Bernstein, and Karl Kautsky first appeared in the *Leipziger Volkszeitung*. It was necessary to put the party on another basis on account of the intentions of certain influential circles in regard to conquest. This had the effect of a bomb. Haase, chairman of the whole party and of the Reichstag faction, had not informed anyone of this intention. In a savage controversy they reproached him with having betrayed the party. The whole machinery of the party was set in motion. Everybody stormed, yelled, and finally forced him to resign.

LEADERS OF YESTERDAY AND TO-DAY

The biggest rumpus was in March, 1916, when the extra budget was brought in; Scheidemann spoke for it in the name of the party. Haase, quite unexpectedly, was against it. He and his friends thought it a matter for the Government. There was an unheard-of scene. The lines were drawn up for battle; mental machine guns limbered for action. On the one side were Dr. David, Keil, and Sachse from the majority; on the other, Haase, Rühle and Henke. "Base coward," "Treachery," and there were even threats of violence. Sachse said to Haase: "You coward, you didn't have the nerve to face the faction. This is a treacherous attack." Haase replied: "The Secretary of State has the courage to doubt whether I am a just representative of the people. One thing I want to say to you and that is this: after twenty months of war, the best patriot is he who works for an understanding, for an end to this war."

This excited debate ended in a general rumpus on the left side of the House. The president was wholly helpless. He could swing the bell, scream, protest — nothing helped. He had to dismiss the sitting.

Under Haase's leadership an organization was formed which later associated itself with the Independent Socialists. The party squabble went on. In public meetings, in the press, and in the Reichstag, this self-destruction continued.

HUGO HAASE

The threads of the revolutionary opposition can be traced far back — from Liebknecht and Rosa Luxemburg to Haase, Cohn, and Dittmann. Haase was soon the confidential man of all those who were dimly striving after the truth — for some way out of this slaughter of human beings, like Beerfelde, Hans Paasche, and the sailors who wanted to start something in 1917. Dr. Michaelis, the Chancellor, and Mr. von Capelle, Secretary of the Navy, accused Haase of high treason in an open session of the Reichstag. But he and Dittmann defended themselves cleverly.

And then the revolution really came. Haase had a thousand threads in his hands — this time they succeeded. The majority of the Social Democrats wanted to form a cabinet including the Haase people and the Democrats, but the Independents objected. They rejected a party union. But they were ready to participate in a purely socialistic cabinet, so that was the way it was arranged.

Two men were put in the same office, a majority man and an Independent — Ebert and Haase at the head of the whole. The one inclined to the right, the other to the left. The Bolshevik-Sparticist group, Liebknecht, Luxemburg, and consorts, daily sought to pull them ever further toward the left.

But Haase remained cool in the midst of the confusion that surrounded him. He would not hear of dictation by the proletariat. He again reflected democratically and was conscious of his duties and responsibilities as a member of the Government.

Militarism, which he had fought against all his life, threatened to lift its head and become dictator in the shape of the executive committee of the workmen and soldiers' councils. Ledebour at the head of this committee attacked his party friends in his usual savage and theatrical manner. Haase did not know which way to turn. He did not wish to fall out with anyone and so he came to no decision. Being a National Liberal he dangled from left to right, hither and thither, hindering the activity of the Goverment by his negative stand. He finally resigned together with Dittmann and Barth. He did not stand the test by fire. Politics means action; he understood only how to criticize. The masses passed over him to the order of the day.

Though he remained the leader of the radical Social Democrats and represented that faction in the National Assembly, the extreme left wing of the party, the noisy battalions of workingmen did not support him. These radical elements clamored for joining hands with the Communists (the German Bolsheviki), Haase held out for a compromise between dictatorship of the proletariat and democratic parliamentarism, but in vain. At the moment when the conflict raging within the party reached its height, a workingman, Voss, made

HUGO HAASE

an attempt upon his life. It has been stated that it was an act of personal revenge. Haase was struck by several revolver shots and mortally wounded. Whatever may have been the ultimate motive behind the deed, it had opened for the party the road to Moscow.

XXX

WILHELM VON WALDOW

Birds of a feather flock together. Dr. Georg Michaelis, the dried-up, bureaucratic, lemon with the sour, sanctimonious halo, fired Herr Tortilowitz von Batocki-Friebe, and called Mr. von Waldow to the head of the War Food Bureau during the dog-days of the year 1917. He who wanted to play the strong man so badly did not resemble Cæsar in this respect. Cæsar loved to have "stout men" about him whose "bald heads slept well o' nights." Herr von Batocki had both a bald head and a thick waist, and we have no reason for presuming that he suffered from insomnia. But in spite of this he was sent to Königsberg, to a quiet retreat in the upper präsidium. A bureaucrat bound in parchment, a yellowed, living document took its place. After the effervescing volubility and ink-slinging of Herr Batocki came the calm and reserve of the over-correct official, the dumb, warning exclamation point. Meager and tall, cold and unapproachable we-must-hold-out — in paragraphs!

The Conservative press rejoiced. At last the uncomfortable Herr Batocki, who always played politics from

WILHELM VON WALDOW

the consumer's point of view and not from the producer's, was left out in the cold, but they forgot that as an East Prussian landowner he was also a producer. The *Deutsche Tageszeitung* wrote: "We would like to warn against the opinion that it needs only an amalgamation of all our food measures in order to insure a better provision for the whole people." The Agrarians had already had enough of the centralization of the food supply and they looked to the new man with hope in their eyes, this man from Stettin, from blessed Pommern. But the leaves of the forest on the Left rustled disapprovingly: "What! Waldow? a man with his political past? One who felt comfortable only in a state of exceptional law-making, who had earned his spurs as an Ostmark fanatic? One who was used to going forward without regard for others?"

The Waldows are genuine Junkers and can trace their ancestry to the thirteenth century. For years they have served their country as officials and officers; two belonged to the Prussian Landtag, Bernhard and Achatz. Naturally they occupied the seats furthest on the right. At the beginning of the century Wilhelm was president of the Government in Königsberg and instituted a strict régime. Bülow stiffened himself with a rigid Ostmark policy at that time; his hobby horse was the anti-Polish policy with which he hoped to pluck a few laurels for himself. At the end of February, 1903, Herr von Bitter resigned from his post as president of the Posen Government because Bülow had found him unsuitable for it; too compliant. Waldow was his successor. "Yon Cassius has a lean and hungry look, he thinks too much; such men are dangerous." But he was just the man for Bülow. In scarcely six months there was a change in the colonization commission. Landrat Blomeyer from Meseritz energetically took over the leadership of the colonization work. The two understood one another excellently. There was a political harmony of souls. Baron von Hammerstein gave the parole in the Landtag in January, 1904. He said: "We are not dealing with opponents who are our equals; we have but to command and they to obey." The Prussian Poles who paid their taxes and served their military term like every other citizen were handled like pariahs on their own inherited land. This was also Waldow's recipe. In this same year the Royal Academy and the Kaiser Friedrich Museum were opened in Posen. An imperial palace in Roman style was built at the entrance to the city as a token of German despotism and power. This was the cultural offensive; the political followed immediately. The so-called language decree opened the joyful nationality battle. Thenceforth Polish children were to receive church instruction in the German language only. The Poles seethed. The clergy protested

WILHELM VON WALDOW

to a man. But it did not help; they went on governing and commanding. A moral conquest must be made under all circumstances. Prussia must be at the front with her Germanizing. In 1907 more than fifty students were dismissed from different Gymnasiums in the province because their brothers and sisters refused to answer in German during religious instructions in the people's school. To the Pole, God is a Pole and the Virgin Mary also, with the mild and gentle features of the black Mother of God of the Jasna Gora in Czenstochau. Shall one speak to her in German? When the Archbishop of Gnesen, Posen, Dr. von Stablewski, died, his chair remained empty for years because the Government rejected all other candidates on the ground that they were suspected of being pro-Polish. The last trump was the expropriation law in 1908. A year later the president invited a number of South German politicians and journalists to a trip through the Ostmark in order proudly to show them the work of colonization that had been done. Fresh, clean, little German villages met the eye of the visitor everywhere, but the silent and tenacious resistance of the Pole was not visible. They did not see the construction of a coöperative trading system going on which was to be an economic weapon in the battle for land.

After the resignation of Prince Bülow the current of events changed slowly. True, Bethmann-Hollweg and the new Minister of Agriculture, Herr von Schoelemer-Leiser, a Catholic, declared that the expropriation law was to be enforced, but we waited long for the first case. In the meantime a new era of reconciliation was dawning. War clouds were beginning to darken the smiling German heavens, and the first command was to set your house in order. All strife and dissension, especially in the neighborhood of the borders, must be done away with: in Posen, West-Prussia, in Alsace-Lorraine, and in Schleswig, all the foreign-speaking parts. In August, 1913, a number of Polish magnates were guests of the Kaiser in the palace at Posen. On the way to the palace many of them were abused by the people. But the new turn of things went on. The times seemed to have returned when, under Caprivi, Herr von Koscielski-Admiralski was *persona gratissima* at the Court and was allowed to kiss the hands of Their Majesties. But perhaps they only seemed to have returned.

Wilhelm von Waldow's rôle was played and grumpily he packed his satchel. Herr Blomeyer had already had to give up his office at head of the colonization commission on account of differences of opinion in regard to the expropriation law. Herr Waldow asked for another sphere of action and got it shortly before the war in the quiet province of Pommern. On account of his icy reserve, he was soon nicknamed the "Frozen Towel" by his official comrades.

WILHELM VON WALDOW

Two years later when everybody was shrieking for a food dictator, he was thought of. But the Left kicked up a row at the first mention of his name and Herr von Batocki won the race. A year later Waldow put his East Prussian colleague out of the running. This highly conservative gentleman with the allurements of power, now entered a queer milieu. He had a Social Democrat as under-secretary. He swallowed this bitter pill. In the council sat a few more Social Democrats, Christians and Hirsch-Dunckers. He accepted this mixed society, too. Finally the Food Bureau was given a Reichstag committee. Even this he worried down. He became State Secretary and at the same time was given the office of Prussian State Food Commissioner, which Herr Michaelis had held until now. This fullness of power which was now laid in his hands was a cooling salve for his ruffled spirits.

Then when he had taken over the office and the press had ceased its ravings, it became remarkably still in his corner of the world. He did not gossip; he worked. Order after order appeared; whole squadrons of paragraphs marched along, but — Batocki's old system remained. The compulsory economic regulations were not changed a bit. The Agrarians soon began to pull long faces and to grumble. Herr von Oldenburg-Januschau, the Don Quixote of the Landowners' League, harnessed his steed more than once for the battle; Dr.

Rösieke, the Ajax of the League, flourished his sword for a brave attack against Batocki's legacy, screaming: "Economics, Horatio, economics!" and brought up a bill in the Reichstag that was to make a breach in the rationing management and give the agrarian possibilities of greater profit. But Herr von Waldow remained hard and immovable like the one-time Landgraf von Thüringen. Now and again he budged a little and granted a little higher price for milk, or for grain, in order to keep up the joy of production. But he failed utterly in the battle against forbidden trafficking in food stuffs. This grew and grew into a mighty weed, although Waldow left no means untried to put a stop to it. He even compelled the Imperial mail service to give up its sublime and lofty secrets. He took the bureau for the prevention of usury to his heart; it became his bodyguard against usurers and illegal traffickers in food.

But the public had grown fatalistic in the meantime. Neither Batocki nor Waldow had stilled their hunger. The one snatched at popularity, the other at paragraphs. Both were conceptions, but conceptions do not fill empty stomachs. The public's temper had gone to the devil on the officially guaranteed but meager daily rations. Herr von Waldow had never had a temper, but nightmares and bad dreams had ceased, for they only come from a full stomach. That at least was one service to the public.

XXXI

RICHARD VON KÜHLMANN

The street was again still where there had been a seething and a boiling for days and weeks. The Piazza had obtained its victim. A dead man lay on the paving stones, a man who, if he had seriously wanted to climb could have climbed to the highest rung of German officialdom — who, as commissioner of the Kaiser and the Bundesrat, could have conducted the affairs of the German nation. But that was all over now, Richard von Kühlmann was officially dead, and so young, only forty-five, and already laid on the shelf at an age when Bismarck had not yet begun to guide the course of Prussia's ship of state.

Was it really all over? As long as Germany had no parliamentary system, as long as there was no continual exchange of strength between ministers and parliamentarians, just so long must our discarded statesmen vanish in the dark depths of some Sans Souci when the winds of disfavor blow in their direction. Very seldom did one ever enter the Reichstag or receive a mission of any sort; Bülow, Posadowsky, and Wermuth were a few of those who reappeared for a fleeting moment on the political surface. The others eked out the rest of their existences on the scanty Royal Prussian pension, either writing memoirs or devoting themselves to music, like Bethmann-Hollweg. When Herr von Kühlmann closed the door of the Foreign Office behind him for the last time, he pushed his chair into a quiet corner and opened a bottle of expensive old wine.

"She caused me more trouble than all the foreign powers or opposing parties at home. The battle against her irritated me more than all the other frictions I had to contend with. She possessed great influence over her husband and sometimes this was not of the best. The king took her part mostly from mere chivalry, even when appearances were against her." So wrote Hermann Hoffmann, the confidential journalist of Friedrichsruh. These were Bismark's words over the Kaiserin Augusta. Herr von Kühlmann, who was reproached with being a gallant, had not merely one or two moral petticoats to contend with, but there were other factors — real "imponderabilities" — which Bismarck understood how to master. For instance, he knew in 1870 and 1871 quite well why he did not stir from general headquarters and leave the field to His Majesty and the Generals. It is charming to read of it to-day. But let us come to the analysis of Kühlmann and his policy:

Kühlmann was a globe-trotter *comme il faut*. He

RICHARD VON KUHLMANN

was born in Constantinople. His father, director of the Anatole railroads, was one of the last to be knighted. He was a citizen of Bavaria and a Catholic. Like all great diplomats, Richard studied law, passed his examinations and devoted himself to foreign service. From attaché to the secretary of the Legation and councilor of the Legation in Petersburg, Teheran, London, Tangiers, Washington, and the Hague, are the various stages of his success. In London he was coworker with Baron von Marschall and Lichnowsky in the effort to bring about a German-English understanding.

During the war he obtained his first responsible post as ambassador to the Hague; here he plucked his laurel wreath at a critical time and was appointed ambassador extraordinary to Turkey in place of Count Wolff-Metternich. He was recalled by Michaelis in 1917, who was a novice in foreign affairs. In quick diplomatic sequence he rushed through the world, saw people and nations, and in time learned to be superior to the situation. This was an advantage and a disadvantage at the same time. An advantage in that he knew how to maintain his distance; a disadvantage in that he undervalued the real, the important. He had something of the manner of a Grand Seigneur whether he wrote, spoke or acted. Everything fell somewhat superciliously from his lips. This was not foolish pride — only a certain aristocratic nonchalance — the indifference of an official who is rich and independent enough to throw the whole mess overboard if they don't like his style. His work did not mean so much to him that it could make him miserable. He did not struggle with principles or powers. Not at all — he played politics — in all seriousness perhaps — like a game of chess, and played with the men who stood behind them. He played and lost finally. He did not stake his name, his children, or his head as did Bismarck, who was acquainted with the idea of dying on a scaffold. He played for the mere charm of playing.

The will to power which lives in every statesman springs from an uplifting, joyous self-assertion — the desire for the best that life affords — mental and spiritual moments that mingle with the intricate waters of esthetic sensibility. Herr Kühlmann could rummage for hours in some antiquity shop, searching for old terra cottas, bits of sculpture, or pictures, but when the hour struck he was on deck surveying the situation and recognizing it too, with keen political intuition. His politics were not as simple as $2 \times 2 = 4$. On the contrary there was an X quantity. This unknown quantity was composed of two factors: when he took over the Foreign Office he faced a number of settled facts, one of which was that the German official peace declarations enjoyed but little credit in foreign countries; the other was, certain influential but not politically respon-

RICHARD VON KÜHLMANN

sible circles hindered the development of his political plans.

One must take these facts into consideration when criticizing his accomplishments. He had the right insight for the fundamental part of a thing, and with fine political instinct could foresee the development of conditions. He soon realized that compromise alone could rescue Germany and all Europe from a catastrophe; he also saw that England alone held the key to the situation. When he tried to grasp it — when instead of that silly Song of Hate he recommended a confidential sounding of the possibilities of peace, there was a regular storm of disapproval from those who wished to continue the war until a decisive victory was won, cost what it may.

And Herr Kühlmann, who might have died a glorious death defending his principles, acted like a schoolboy caught stealing jam. He began to explain — he didn't mean it that way, but so and so. There was a stammering and a kotowing before Count Westarp after the Chancellor had handed the Secretary of State his walking papers. This was how he died — a faithful servant of the powers whose nerves were stronger than his own.

At the conclusion of peace with Russia in Brest-Litowsk did he follow the dictation of others? What a great political work might have been accomplished — the first steps toward a universal and honorable compromise. This great opportunity was disregarded for the sake of a bit of land, and the problem was solved instead with tedious conflicts and half truths such as giving the right of self-government if they would submit to annexation, etc. The Brest-Litowsk peace was a botch, a hindrance to future understanding, a retreat before the fist of General Hoffmann. The Bucharest peace was more conclusive and consequent — the details of the treaty with Roumania were cleverly thought out; Kühlmann was not blinded by hate or revenge but went to work soberly and unprejudiced like a business man.

On August 22, 1917, in his speech to the Reichstag as representative of the German people for the first time, he proclaimed Might and Right as the foundations of German politics.

His policy rested only upon the one pillar — Might — in Brest as well as in Bucharest; when he showed an inclination to base his policy upon Right, they chased him out. Called to General Headquarters for explanation, he ran against a prejudice, a mood that was like coming out of the hot sun into an ice cellar.

Thereupon he sat himself down and wrote out his resignation. The fourth Secretary of State since the war began now entered upon his duties: Jagow, Zimmermann, Kühlmann, and now Admiral von Hintze.

XXXII

PAUL FUHRMANN

After the collapse of Bülow's block, when Center and Conservatives paired off, the National Liberal party, the middle piece of the block, swayed toward the Left. War to the knife was declared against the Landowner's League, three representatives whose leanings toward the right were well known, were thrown out of the party. In this way Count Oriola and Baron Heyl zu Herrnsheim, the leather king of Worms, were thrown into the arms of the Progressives. Liberals on both sides founded the Hansa Bund for trade, professions, and industry; laid a trap, not unsuccessfully, for the fragile Middle, and formed a league for the approaching elections. Social democracy was the silent partner whom the National Liberals had to call on in their battle against the Center, although one really could not speak to them on the street. That was in 1912 in Saarbrücken; and now Philipp Scheidemann was chosen vice-president of the new Reichstag with the assistance of the National Liberal party. In Rhineland-Westphalia, where the National Liberal captains of industry (the very antipodes of social democracy) have their seat, they wrinkled their brows and went wild when Herr Scheidemann, who had gotten onto the president's seat with the crutches of the National Liberal party, refused to do his courtly duties, namely, to be presented to the Kaiser. That was an impudence; republican anti-monarchism, etc. The German kingdom threatened to go to pieces. At the second ballot the National Liberals meekly placed their votes in the right place and Scheidemann was out of it. Privy Councillor Dove sat in his place and filled the vacancy in the presidential chair with stoical calm. Two Progressives and one National Liberal now sat there. Three representatives from two parties which, taken both together, did not come up to the numbers of the Social Democrats.

The capitalists of the National Liberals kept on intriguing and trying to get the Hansa Bund on their own particular track. President Riesser gave in at first, but later kicked up a row and the industrial captains gave notice, Dr. Rötger at their head. They were out. This was the first wedge in the Liberal alliance. The second was directed against the National Liberal party itself.

Who was at the bottom of this politically unclean business, seeking to undermine the party and laying his explosives everywhere? Surely someone who belonged to the right wing of the party and whose interest it was to make that wing the authoritative one. Far

PAUL FUHRMANN

from it! It was one from the Left side who bit on the capitalists' bait: Herr Paul Fuhrmann, member of the Landtag from the sixth Arnsberger voting district, general secretary of the National Liberal party, and acquainted with all the secrets of the Berlin central bureau where he worked. The captains of industry persuaded him, the confidential man of the whole National Liberal organization, to betray the party in order to form an organization of their own, and Herr Fuhrmann, who could have bought a baronial estate with the money of his former wife, accepted the offer!

After this step, Dr. Weber, a prominent member of the business committee of the party, wrote on the 28th of June, 1912:

"I can think of no greater felony than that a man like you, who has really been kept in office by the support of Bassermann and myself, should now betray us in this manner, not merely in order to ruin the position of Herr Bassermann but to disrupt the whole party which I have tried so hard to keep together.

"Immediately after my arrival in Berlin I asked repeatedly at your office if you were not to be seen. Herr Breithaupt (the other general secretary) has done the same but always in vain. Thereupon I questioned the staff and discovered the following facts:

"1. Contrary to your usual habit of appearing at eleven or twelve o'clock at the bureau, since taking up the work of the new organization you have appeared for days and weeks as early as nine o'clock every morning in order to finish work for the other league. Was it not a matter of course that you should give up your work in the central bureau as soon as you had accepted a rival undertaking?

"2. For days you have been studying the secret book which is really only for the use of the business committee. Until you accepted the new position you never opened this book. Since then you have questioned the staff repeatedly in the attempt to obtain exact information in regard to the number of party friends and contributions.

"3. You have occupied the ladies in the office with writing out addresses which were to serve in winning members for your new party.

"4. You tried to persuade the ladies to furnish you with still more addresses until Sunday morning when Herr Kalthoff returned and put an end to the further work of the ladies.

"5. You asked for and received the organization's handbook in order to increase your address material for the new organization.

"I have confirmed these facts and after doing so I do not hesitate to utter my opinion to the business committee. I maintain that your actions are shameful, that it was shocking for you to remain in our bureau

PAUL FUHRMANN

after being employed by the other. I have protested against this and am ready to take the consequences of my actions."

Was this sufficient? Not for Herr Fuhrmann. He continued to meet Mr. Weber as if nothing had happened. Herr Bassermann called his conduct the "most indecent he had ever seen in his life." Herr Fuhrmann remained a member of the party and representative of the people in the Prussian Landtag. He bought off Breithaup's son, who deserted from the army, for eight hundred marks. He did this for intimate reasons, in memory of the father and the founding of the old-national liberal organization. He should really destroy the intimacies of his political doings before they fall into other hands, for they are very embarrassing. Old Herr Breithaup's mouth is closed forever; his tongue is silenced out there under the grass. But there is much more that could be said — personal things. But we have to do with the politician not with the private citizen.

Herr Fuhrmann's actions cannot be excused on the plea of youth. He has long since passed the age of foolishness. After leaving the Stolper Gymnasium he attended the Berlin University for several semesters, studying history and the history of art.

When the war broke out he transformed himself, like a good many German industries. Now he joined that band of nameless editors in order to fight against the National Liberal party for old-nationalism, *i. e.,* for the captains of industry. The *Berliner Neuesten Nachrichten,* which for a long time was not able either to live or to die, and then for a time combined with the *Deutsche Zeitung,* offered him a platform for his activities after it had been financially renovated. The party got rid of the *Neuesten Nachrichten* more than once, but they could not get rid of Herr Fuhrmann; he stuck like a cocklebur and went on stirring up a row against the party. When the six economic leagues published a memorial in 1915, advocating extensive annexations, it was Fuhrmann who opened his mouth the widest and wrote and carped against Bethmann-Hollweg, who kept his head clear. When the Fatherland party was called into existence he was one of the first to join the ranks as a propagandist. And so powerful was his speech in a Berlin propaganda meeting that the audience resented the fact that some war invalids present, dared to remonstrate, and beat them up. Herr Fuhrmann, who let himself be advertised by the bureau of the Langtag, Herr Fuhrmann, the prototype of a home warrior, stood on the platform and beamed at this scene. It was the triumph of his life.

In the Landtag he was the soul of the right wing of the National Liberal party. He and Herr Hirsch, the Essen general secretary, both had a

PAUL FUHRMANN

finger in the pie. If the faction showed symptoms of leaning toward the left, quickly he let loose the National Liberal industrials' mutiny against the liberal element. Almost always he succeeded, but fortunately, not at the franchise reform. After everything had been tried in vain to convert them all to the franchise reform, the party finally separated and worked independently: the right and the left. And Herr Fuhrmann, who had once in Stendal called the three-class system the most shameful he could think of, now worked in the front line to help forge the franchise compromise with the Conservatives. Again he betrayed the party and with it one of it's most prominent members, Dr. Friedberg, vice-president of the Prussian State Ministry and champion of equal suffrage, and when the great pow-wow came, all were suddenly converted.

This is the way Herr Fuhrmann looks. Herr Fuhrmann, who likes to play the great moralist, whose speeches drip with German spirit, with German character, and German will to power.

XXXIII

GEORG GRAF VON HERTLING

Count Hertling was called to the head of the Government in his seventy-fifth year, an age when the average official has retired to enjoy his pension in peace and quiet. "If I have decided to accept the difficult and responsible position of Imperial Chancellor in these stormy times," he said with a slight tone of resignation, "if I overlook the objection to my age, it is only in the conviction that it is my duty to sacrifice myself for my fatherland." Only he who is above ambition, who realizes that we are not in this world to live for ourselves but to live for others, can speak in this manner. Once before in 1917, when Bethmann-Hollweg was forced out of office, Count Hertling was called upon to take his place, but he refused on account of his age and the fact that there were others eagerly waiting for the post. But the experiment with someone from the "bullrun of bureaucracy," to quote Bismarck, was not a success; the entre act with Michaelis somewhat tragicomically came to a surprisingly quick end. This time Count Hertling felt obliged to accept. It was a great sacrifice for a man of his age to make, physically as well as psychologically.

GEORG GRAF VON HERTLING

He was fragile and so shortsighted that he had to be accompanied when he went out. One forgot his bodily weaknesses when one heard him speaking, fluently and brilliantly, in the Reichstag. Life, energy, and will, flared up in this insignificant-looking little man, and his eyes began to sparkle behind the thick spectacles. A tinge of red flushed the small, white-bearded, pointed face that looked so much like that of a mouse. I once asked a well-known foreign diplomat what impression Count Hertling made upon him. He answered, smiling: "A charming old man."

"And what did you get out of him?" I continued.

"He told me a lot, but he always got around the things I really wanted to know."

He is not one you can entice on thin ice—not one who heedlessly announces his determinations. If you observe him at a sitting in the Bundesrat you will probably think he is too tired to follow the proceedings. Silently he sits there seemingly sunk in thought. But whenever the thread of discourse threatens to go astray he quickly interferes; in clear, pointed words he brings the theme back to the point.

He is thoroughly conservative but conditions have driven him to opposition. Even when he had reached the highest rung of the ladder he abandoned the views of yesterday and to-day, and not without hesitation he ushered in a part of new German politics.

LEADERS OF YESTERDAY AND TO-DAY

If I am to paint a spiritual portrait of him I must not loosely string a few superficial, political events together, but must begin at the beginning of his mental and spiritual development, with philosophy, which saturates his whole political doings.

He began to teach in the university at Bonn in 1867, but got no further than lecturer. Thirteen years later he became professor, but only under-professor, although he had written a number of significant works on philosophy. But in this period of Kultur war he was a suspect — he held fast to the teachings of the Vatican and was faithful to the church in her battle with the state. Later, as professor of philosophy in Munich, he was less a pioneer of new systems than a historian, a critic of the old. His dogmatic, theological narrowness forbade it. Catholic Christianity places a supermundane, personal God at the beginning of everything. The world is an act of his creative all-power, and the predestination of mankind lies in the Beyond. This transcendental problem is already settled and philosophy has nothing to do but formulate it, as Hertling once said in an article on the church-father, Augustine. He settled this affair with Plato and the Neoplatonists, and occupied himself with Aristotle.

If you wish to understand Hertling as a politician you must not overlook this Catholic-scholastic education which tends toward a smooth and supple dialectic.

GEORG GRAF VON HERTLING

While still a lecturer at Bonn in 1875, he was a successful candidate for the Reichstag and fought with Windhorst and Reichensperger against the Iron Chancellor, who was trying to break the backbone of the Center and the Vatican. A year later he helped to found the Görres society in Coblenz for the study of science, including political and national, in Catholic Germany. With fine feeling for the needs of the people, he paid especial attention to social politics. This was his specialty at that time. More than once Bismarck invited him to a conference on social matters. In 1883 he bared his heart to him on the question of the unhappy Kultur war. Clever and tactful Hertling met him half way, assuring him that even the Center representatives longed for the harmony of a church and political peace. Gradually Center and Chancellor were again at sword's points over the new tariff and economic politics. This noisy clash ceased at times, but behind the political scenes the Catholic church did not budge an inch. In the acts of the Görres society one can read the following: "The state is naturally subordinate to the temporary and beneficial organization of the church."

Notwithstanding this the Center continued to be on friendly terms with free-thinkers and Social Democrats — the most pronounced representatives of tolerance — with Richter and Grillenberger — in order to fight Bismarck's exceptional law-making.

LEADERS OF YESTERDAY AND TO-DAY

After Lieber's death Hertling became chief of the Center faction, party diplomat, and let the Government buy his approval for the military and naval propositions. This cool business policy which even Bülow had not ventured on in the beginning, brought the Center the gradual rescindment of the Jesuit laws, but it later led to a rupture between them and the Government, in 1906. This did not last long — the conservative-liberal block went to pieces on the finance reform bill. Stronger than ever the Center party emerged from its temporary isolation. Just at the right moment they could throw their political weight in the scales when Pope Pius X issued his challenge to all modern movements which threatened to interfere with the revenues of the state. Hertling's rôle as intermediary was not small. In 1912, when Podewil's ministry in Bavaria went to pieces in a conflict with the Center, Hertling was trusted with the formation of a new cabinet. The Bavarian Center majority became an official government's party over night. Thus the first parliamentary régime entered the German federal states although none of the participators liked to admit it.

Hertling now occupied a responsible position; he automatically became chairman of the Bundesrat commission for foreign affairs, and obtained a deep insight into international politics. Bavaria's national influence grew tremendously; it had never been so strong in the

GEORG GRAF VON HERTLING

past as in the five years ending 1917. Bethmann-Hollweg depended upon his support and it was but natural he should be thought of when the Chancellor resigned.

He did not let the Kaiser appoint him to the chancellorship directly, but got in touch with the majority parties — the Center, Independents, and Social Democrats. He agreed upon a positive working program and called leading parliamentarians into the Government from these parties who had once formed an opposing majority in the Reichstag. This was the first step toward a parliamentary system. This was his permanent service to the nation. He remained true to the program agreed upon. In the midst of the hottest battle for equal suffrage in Prussia he declared he would stand or fall with this question. But faithfulness did not win out. Political life began to slump — the suffrage reform did not budge from the spot, military rulers became more and more impudent, the majority began to grumble, the Social Democrats announced their mistrust, the progressives withdrew their support, and at last the Center dropped him. The Chancellor went to Headquarters and came back a dead man. The Kaiser accepted his resignation. The way was clear for popular Government; the historical document was signed by Count Hertling himself. He made a brilliant retreat.

He handled foreign politics as he had once handled philosophy: fatalistically; he bent to the powers that were stronger than he. Originally he attempted to take the German answer to the Pope's note as a basis for his war and peace policy. This answer was a relinquishment of thoughts of annexation or compensation. However, he slowly adapted himself, under all sorts of rhetorical reservations, to the new military atmosphere which daily and hourly surrounded him. He forgot the question of St. Augustine, whom he had formerly praised, forgot the remark of the church-father in his "God's Nation," a treatise on the Roman Empire; if it were really great or praiseworthy to sow war without end, to subjugate independent peoples, and out of this wreckage of destroyed freedom and independence, to erect a mighty monument to ambition? Step by step he retreated before those who believed Germany's future to be insured only by annexations. It cost him much trouble to cover this retreat with ambiguous phrases. In the shape of a German-Russian peace treaty he left a legacy for the German people whose far-reaching political significance will only be realized later.

He did not fail to make attempts to come to a peaceful understanding with the Western powers but he succeeded no better than his predecessors. He waited for things to approach him in order to reduce possibilities of friction to the lowest point. He remained quiet and became more and more the executor of other people's wills. If he accomplished anything at all by opposing the military authorities, seen in the light of day, it was but a meager compromise. The sliest fox would rather have a bird in hand than two in the bush. And so he sat behind the large mirrors in the aristocratic, baroque, dreamy, old Chancellor palace gazing at the round bed of rhododendrons, roses, and pansies, and waited for the long-desired guest who must come sometime — for peace.

But Count Hertling waited in vain. He died in Munich before the guest arrived.

XXXIV

ROBERT FRIEDBERG

One who has sold his soul to politics is Robert Friedberg, a professor, national economist, parliamentarian by profession, and for a year minister without portfolio. He stands in the frame of National Liberalism, a changing framework? No, a one-sided exclusive picture that sits fast in its frame.

Dr. Friedberg, who studied in Leipzig and lectured in Halle on political science, did not make much of a record scientifically. That was not his territory. He wrote one or two books on exchange dues and public finances. But he had been politically active for many years. In 1886, at the age of thirty-five, he entered the House of Representatives and never came out of it. Halle sent him first and then Remscheid-Lennep. Only once, and that temporarily, did he enter the Reichstag. It was the year when Prince Hohenlohe's tired hands held the reins of state.

He has a stately appearance, is wholly professor, has a small, square-cut, grayish beard, wears spectacles on a rather thick nose, has a thick head of hair, reddish cheeks, and a slender body on elastic legs. He is almost always clothed in a frock coat and yet there is no trace of formality about him. He is always friendly, always courteous — even gives his hand to Adolph Hoffmann in greeting, his antipode from the extreme Left. He is always on deck when the political oar is to be shoved onto the right track. It is a pleasure to hear him speak; without a trace of pathos, always objective, his words are like a string of pearls. He is ready of wit and not to be discomposed.

He is a piece of good National Liberal tradition. His interests are concentrated exclusively on Prussia. He has always been a master at this. The party division was a good one: Bassermann controlled the kingdom, Friedberg the state of Prussia. One did not get in the other's range. Before he took up a parliamentary career he had already done service for the party. On party days he was the mediator and knew how to win people with his friendly manner. Even to-day he is above everything else a tactician. In the Landtag, when the budget estimates were discussed, his speeches were always the *pièce de résistance*. He fairly swelled in finance and tax questions, carefully touching upon the railroad compensation funds which had so often helped the budget on its legs, and disapproving of the additional income-tax provision, and the policy of the minister of finance.

He did not try to conceal the fact that he was a

professional politician, since he laid his professorship on the shelf. In his great speech against the Upper House in March, 1917, the day of the Russian revolution, when he recommended a reform of the First Chamber, he also ironically referred to a reproach against professional parliamentarism which had been dropped by the Conservatives: "The remarks about professional parliamentarians have a comical as well as a serious side," he said. "What advantages has a parliamentarian in Germany? I know of but one and that is the consciousness of having fulfilled his duties to the best of his ability. When a man, financially independent, takes upon himself the burdens of Parliament as his life's task, when he tries to keep up the traditions of the House and relieve his overburdened colleagues who have other professions, that effort deserves something better than a mere mockery of professional parliamentarism." And then as a counter blow he said that the statements made by the House were not compatible with the constitution. Under a roar of applause from the left of the House he concluded his speech with the remark: "When one takes the widest conception possible of the Government, including the lawmaking department, then one may say that all people have the Government and the Parliament they deserve. But the Prussian people really have not deserved an Upper Chamber of this sort."

ROBERT FRIEDBERG

In the meantime Dr. Friedberg has become minister, vice-president of the Prussian ministry, the first parliamentary minister in Prussian Germany to retain his representative mandate and the first to leave the Government table and give his vote with his party comrades. He was really a reform-minister, the franchise hero. But all his versatility and business knowledge were not enough to budge the Right; they were obdurate and the right wing of the National Liberals, the Fuhrmann and Hirsch consorts, gave up their friendship for him at the command of the capitalists. In the battle for equal suffrage he passed from one defeat to another. The Landtag alone rejected the equality principle twice in the commission and four times in the plenum. But Herr Friedberg still hoped, although, naturally, the Upper Chamber refused to follow. Was he waiting for a miracle? Why did he not dissolve the House and write out a new election asked the Left. But the miracle came — when it was too late. Friedberg's optimism was justified.

The military situation changed all at once to Germany's disadvantage. Bulgaria surrendered, we asked for a truce, and the Conservatives gave in. All resistance against the franchise bill was given up. The Upper Chamber and the Landtag swallowed it as best they might. On the other hand, Dr. Friedberg and the Left with him, crawled under the caudinian yoke of the Center's denominational "assurance."

He should not have been a National Liberal. In 1892 the party smothered Baron von Zedlitz's Prussian Folks school law. Fourteen years later, under Friedberg, they participated in the confessionalizing of the Folks school which, according to the will of the Center, were now to have a constitutional guarantee. In the franchise question he went another way. Originally he was opposed to the thought of equal suffrage and was enthusiastic for a plural system according to age, education, and property. Then he condensed the direct and secret vote and finally, under the pressure of war conditions, he was converted to equal suffrage. Formerly the opponent of a parliamentary system, he now became a parliamentarian indeed. The right wing of the party could not forget this. What did all his services count for now; they despised him as a deserter.

To be sure he was always rather a suspect. In the quarrel of the old-National Liberals with the rest of the party he stuck to the Central organization but had a smile of forgiveness for the young Liberals. He understood how to rise above petty differences; after the death of Bassermann he became chairman of the Central committee and in time he was the party trademark. It was due to his agitation that the model press bureau was founded, that yearly spread millions of

ROBERT FRIEDBERG

National Liberal papers among the voting masses. He played party politics like a piano, in sharps and in flats, runs and trills; just as quickly with the right in the bass as with the left in the treble, but he was long in finding the one melody which meant the realization of equal suffrage in Prussia.

In the fall of 1918, he appeared in Prince Max's war cabinet as the confidential man of the National Liberals. Then he disappeared in the deluge like all the rest of his colleagues, when the revolutionary waves broke over Germany. But he emerged again as a democratic candidate at the election for the National Assembly after the National Liberal party had gone to pieces, was elected, and became the leader of the party.

XXXV

HANS GEORG VON BEERFELDE

One day in the summer of 1917, my telephone rang at an unusual hour.

"Dombrowski speaking," I answered.

"Beerfelde," replied a deep voice, "Captain von Beerfelde."

I had never heard the name before.

"Could I see you in regard to a pressing matter? It is very important."

"Certainly, but what is it about?"

"Something must be done. Anything. It is high time."

"Yes, but what am I to understand by that?"

"The whole political situation, the absolute necessity of an immediate peace; the consequences of the Russian revolution — We must speak of these things and decide upon some sort of action."

"May I ask who is at the back of all this?"

"I am. The Chancellor is informed of the state of affairs; we must make it clear to the military authorities. A number of other gentlemen have already promised to come to the Café Rheingold to discuss the situation: Privy Councillor X, Director Y, Editor Z, etc."

"All right, I'll come."

Punctually I arrived at the Rheingold on the afternoon of the same day. When I entered the cozy little front room an officer and a very well-known scholar were already seated in the leather chairs and were in the midst of a lively conversation. The officer jumped up hastily and impulsively offered his hand.

"Beerfelde is my name."

"I am Dombrowski."

He was a dapper, erect, somewhat undersized officer, with the Iron Cross, first class, under his left breast, an intelligent face, brown and weather-beaten, a short mustache, thick, copper-colored hair, trimmed like a hedge, as if the barber had imagined himself to be a Le Notre, the celebrated gardener of the baroque period; heavy browns and — such eyes! Could they bore through one at a glance? They were the eyes of a man accustomed to command, a man used to action — or were they only the eyes of a man carried away by an idea?

A curious mixture, aristocratic, energetic, dauntless.

Soon there were ten or twelve of us, twelve men whose names were all well-known in Berlin intellectual circles.

The Geheimrat called the meeting to order at the request of Captain von Beerfelde. He excused the absence of two professors, and gave a short outline of the political situation. It was about the time of the secret sittings of the Reichstag committees, during the weeks when the battle against Bethmann-Hollweg raged its worst and the peace resolution was nearing its fulfillment.

One groped in political darkness and the Geheimrat declared another winter of war must be prevented by all means.

"Something must be done," the Captain completed, requesting those present to make some suggestions.

An embarrassing pause ensued. They looked at one another almost beseechingly.

Gradually a discussion arose but it crept along tediously. One suggested informing Hindenburg and Ludendorff of the exact state of affairs at home. Of course the Kaiser should know, too. They thought Bethmann-Hollweg was already informed. Herr von Harnack and the Captain had spoken with him the day before.

The others objected to this procedure. How could one approach Hindenburg, and moreover what was one to say positively if one did get an audience? Another pause.

The whole discussion seemed at an end.

One skeptic doubted the whole story.

At this moment the Captain sprung up, seized his

portfolio and notebook, pounded the table with his fist, and cried out: "I see the gentlemen will only talk. I am going to act. If I have to stake my head for it! Good-day, gentlemen!" And he marched out with heavy tread. For a time we stared at one another in painful silence. Finally our gaze concentrated on the scholar.

He was embarrassed. "I perceive," he began at last, "that you wish some sort of explanation from me. But I cannot give you one. The Captain visited me yesterday, urged my attendance at this meeting in the light of a moral duty, and mentioned the names of other gentlemen who would be present. I did not think I could very well refuse under the circumstances. He is, after all, a man of position: soldier, Iron Cross, first class officer of the Staff, noble . . . Well, I came without knowing what he really wanted of me."

A second repeated the same story: sudden visit, Iron Cross, noble, officer of the Staff, etc.

The third, the fourth, and all the rest.

Everybody laughed but nevertheless felt somewhat ashamed.

Weeks passed by; the Captain's name slipped from my mind. Suddenly I received a visit from him. In a few words he recalled the meeting at the Rheingold and asked if I, too, had shaken my head over him.

"No," I replied.

"Why not?"

"You were the only one who really wanted to act; the others did not know what to say. I was impressed by the tragedy of the moment although I did not know what you really wanted of me."

"I trust you. I have new evidence that something must be done. Do you know the Prince Lichnowsky pamphlet?"

"I have heard of it."

"Would you like to have one?"

"Yes. Where did you get it, Captain?"

"Someone loaned it to me. I said to myself: This must be made public so that everyone will have a chance to know the truth."

"Yes, but all that is very serious . . ."

"I have twelve copies. Here is one."

Once again I saw Herr von Beerfelde but only for a moment. A few weeks later I was called before the court and requested to give up the Lichnowsky booklet. I had to sign an affidavit that I had not spread any copies of this book nor had any printed. All the others who possessed a copy were haled into court and they thought they had all the copies at last but — the last man summoned confessed that he had ordered and distributed about five hundred copies. They had gone the way of all other disclosures.

In the meantime Beerfelde came into conflict with

HANS GEORG VON BEERFELDE

his superiors, who were supposed to have forbidden him to have anything to do with politics. He was court-martialed, but because there was no such order to be found, they had to let him go. While he was in prison awaiting trial, he brooded more than ever. From out his world of thought came the incessant cry: "You must act! Do something!" He wrote to Ludendorff and Hindenburg: "Germany's fate during and after the war depends largely upon whether we truthfully represent a truthful cause. Although we win the battle we are preparing the way for our own downfall in any other case; we would never fulfill our mission in the world. With truth alone can we conquer the enemies at home and abroad." A grown-up child — an enthusiast who sees life only from the perspective of a cloud-dweller? Perhaps. But at the same time this mystic dreamer is a man who must and will act.

His goal is not clear; it is blurred and misty. In this respect he differs from Thomas Stockmann, whom the "compact majority" called an enemy of the people. He knew exactly how to convert truth to deeds.

But Beerfelde danced around like a will-o'-the-wisp. He did not know exactly what he should do, and finally stood on the periphery of Independent Social Democracy. He began to form connections that brought him under suspicion of having had something to do with the Berlin strike movement at the end of January,

1918. Compromising letters, circulars and papers were found and confiscated. In short, he was charged with having transgressed paragraph 89 of the criminal code. Treason . . .

Is the world foolish, or is he who was led by the purest humanitarian motives, only to be helplessly entangled in life's net? Do we damn Michael Kohlhaas, who was similarly tortured by the necessity for action — who, seeking justice, went to extremes and at last tripped over himself?

To the judge, the sentence. And it is the duty of the private citizen not to interfere with the proceedings of the law.

This article was written at the beginning of April, 1918, but the Commandant forbade its publication. It would have been too awful if the world discovered that an officer no longer believed in the imperialistic-militaristic ideals.

Now that the revolutionary wave has cast Captain von Beerfelde, a. D (*ausser Dienst* — out of service) to the top, making him for a few days one of the most important men of Germany, I again fetch out my manuscript together with a whole mountain of Beerfelde material — articles and letters to the Kaiser, to the Crown Prince, to Hindenburg, etc.

When the Captain returned from the field, over-irritated and excited, his eyes fell upon the yet unknown

HANS GEORG VON BEERFELDE

Lichnowsky memorial. He had seen the unveiled image of truth and it scorched his soul. In his despair — in the hope that all they had said was not true,— the Lichnowskys, Dr. Muehlon, Fernau, and the others — he wrote to the Kaiser on Easter Sunday, 1918: "In the name of a betrayed people I demand that every document and agreement made between us and Austria-Hungary before the war and which do not appear in our white book, now be made public. I demand . . ."

More shocking than all these attempts to clear the situation was his legal complaint made on the 11th of September while awaiting trial in the Berlin military prison. Out of a martyred soul welled forth this cry:

"Those who know me, all my former superior officers and comrades, can testify that I have always stood for a clear and clean situation, that I have hated every lazy compromise no matter what advantages it might bring me.

"I want nothing more than that truth and justice, the greatest of all powers, should build an open road for our army and our people toward a blessed and noble future. According to the Bible: 'Justice lifteth up a people but the sins of injustice casteth them down!' Why are not such words heeded? Have we the right to call ourselves a Christian folk, a Christian State? I know that everyone of my subordinates in the field would subscribe to these words. There will be great surprises in store for those who do not follow a policy of truth when the army returns from the field. The best elements of this army are filled with a ruthless desire for truth. For truth alone do German men shed their blood. Everything else will be ruthlessly cast aside. You here at home should take heed. When I left my battalion I promised my men if I were no longer needed at the front I would do my best to provide 'good quarters' at home. And I intend to keep this promise to the best of my ability.

"Lichnowsky uttered his convictions before the new faction in the Landtag, but they called him an excitable fool and a dupe. The majority rejected his illuminating ideas, and no memorial, no argument, could induce them to change their minds. Where is the person who can listen to the warning voice of Cassandra unshaken, or without asking: Can this be true? But it really seems as if no one will listen. Then they must be made to feel and it will be terrible. I am almost mad with despair in the vain endeavor to spread the truth. Now I stand before the court. Will they listen to me there? I trust they will; that is why I do not defend myself in the usual manner. I shall accuse and lay my soul bare before them. One thing only I ask: Examine, investigate, prove, and do not rest until the truth is found! I have an enormous amount of material to place at your disposal. Whoever will take the trouble to examine it will be able to see clearly. It was just the same with me. I was firmly convinced of the justice of our cause; I can furnish hundreds of proofs of my enthusiasm in the beginning — until instinctively I felt there was something wrong at home. And then came the bitter illumination. I was nigh unto despair. Since I saw what I have seen there is but one road for me — bear witness for the truth, if I must die for it in order that our unsuspecting people may not be ruined.

"I do not write this for effect — it is the cold, sober, and holy truth and unchangeable resolve."

The court was not able to bring in a verdict — revolution rattled on the doors of the prison house where he sat and presented him his freedom. In a trice he was at the top. On the 9th of November he took charge of the almighty executive committee of the Workmen and Soldiers' Councils. Now he was to stand his test. But in three days he was dismissed. He had shown himself too stormy for the systematic work of organization.

He was swallowed up again in the nothingness of everyday. Unawares he stepped into the waves — will they ever cast him up again? In the meanwhile he is stranded at a sanatorium.

XXXVI

PAUL VON HINTZE

One day I received an invitation from His Excellency the Secretary of the Foreign Office, Herr von Hintze, Wilhelmstrasse 76, first floor. The rooms were well known to me. In the modest vestibule lie the two sphinxes on their stone postaments eying every intruder good-humoredly. The conference room on the first floor makes a simple, virtuous impression. No silken wall paper, no soft carpets, no heavy damask curtains before the windows. A green-covered, horseshoe-shaped table occupies almost the whole of the small room. On the left wall is a life-size portrait of Wilhelm II in his thirtieth year; on the right, Kaiser Friedrich. Near it the well-known marine tables from His Majesty, dating from the time of the navy enthusiasm. In a window niche, a huge globe. With the exception of a bookcase that is all the furniture in the room.

A few legation councillors, active and inactive clerks, an under-Secretary of State, and lastly the Secretary himself. Subject of discussion was politics, naturally confidential.

Herr von Hintze opened the meeting with a long résumé of the situation. A fresh, energetic man,

PAUL VON HINTZE

rather short, very active and full of inner unrest like a distant, rumbling, volcano. Externally calm, with a trace of superiority. Speaks genially and yet a bit condescendingly. Likes to have his listeners believe that he regards everything *sub specie aeterni*. He knows people and knows that they like to be deceived; knows people from all over the world, for he has been thrown from pillar to post most of his life.

The two large, brown eyes wander regularly from left to right and from right to left during his conversation; he likes to have the whole of his little audience under control. And he wants to make an impression, not merely with the subject itself but also with his treatment of it. He speaks in choice phrases without pauses, periods or exclamation points — smooth and rounded like a book. Not a single clause is wasted; one sentence follows another in well-ordered array. He blows every little grain of stylistic unevenness from the filigree of his conversation, making every moment some remark, some insinuation, some twist, designed to illustrate his literary knowledge, which is not exactly modern.

He is no self-sufficient aristocrat; he is a man of strict self-discipline, who has labored to acquire what he possesses. He makes nothing of family connections, or material possessions — and has boldly remained a bachelor to the present day.

Fate did not favor him externally. When he was still in the navy, people said he looked like the Kaiser's state coachman. And now he's driving the Imperial German National coach. But those who made fun of him secretly respected him all the same. They called him the crazy, clever, industrious, and ambitious Hintze. He was soon an all round man, indefatigably active, and absolutely inconsiderate when it came to reaching a goal he had set for himself as the right one. Of course a goal always lies in a direct line with one's own advantages. He showed backbone as a naval officer without dispensing entirely with diplomatic cunning. On the contrary he was especially good at this. As first officer on board the *Kaiser Wilhelm II,* he thought he had discovered a sort of indolence among the younger set. He went after them with pitch and sulphur, naturally making a good many enemies, but he did not let that influence him any. He had no prejudices, was too much a man of the world for this. When one of his comrades had to leave the service on account of a mésalliance, the others, according to narrow-minded custom, concluded not to send a wedding present. Hintze, as crew senior, protested against such antiquated opinions, and the present was sent.

In 1882 he entered the navy as cadet. At the examination he won first place, which he continued to keep. Admiral von Truppel, later governor of Kiaochow and a very strict disciplinarian, was his officer. It was not easy for Hintze and he was at one time ready to leave the service. But his energy overcame all hindrances. For three years he gondoliered round the world on board the cruiser frigate *Prinz Adelbert*. When he returned in 1885, he was sub-lieutenant. The way to fame was open. But the way was long and fame let him wait for a considerable length of time. Several commands of no particular importance followed. It seemed as if they had not recognized Hintze's talents. He had to drill recruits, attend torpedo practice, and a lot more of the same sort. Naturally this did not content him. He entered the Naval Academy and remained there from 1894 to 1896. The navy hubbub was just beginning. While his comrades were enjoying themselves, Hintze worked like a horse learning one language after another and gathering all sorts of information. He dressed well and did not despise amusements, but he was always within bounds, never in high spirits.

In 1896 he arrived at the first stage of his ambition; on the 8th of April he was made Lieutenant-Captain of the naval staff. His upward climb proceeded rapidly. Two years later he was Flag-Lieutenant of the East Asiatic cruiser squadron. His chief was Vice-Admiral von Diederichs. For the first time, if only for a moment, Hintze's name went the rounds of the world.

It was during the Dewey affair at Manila, in the summer of 1898, when Admiral von Diederichs anchored in Manila Bay. The Admiral sent Hintze to Dewey to remonstrate against the threatened searching of two German war vessels. " Young man, do you tell me that means war ? " exclaimed Dewey. In spite of his thirty-six years Hintze looked very young at that time, with his smooth-shaven face. As everyone knows there was nothing to the conflict but a noisy press campaign. Prince Heinrich took von Diederich's place as commander of the cruiser squadron and Hintze became his staff officer. He left the *Kaiser Wilhelm* and went on board the *Deutschland*. The commander was Captain Müller (later chief of the navy cabinet) who enjoyed a reputation similar to Hintze's in naval circles. Two gentlemen of eminent cunning thus met on board ship. They were not congenial, partly on account of the Prince. But they did the cleverest thing under the circumstances, concluded peace, swore eternal friendship for better or for worse. This compact has been cherished and has been the better for both parties concerned.

In 1901 Hintze came home, was promoted to corvet Captain and come on board the *Kaiser Wilhelm II* as commander. For many years he had not been in active service and gradually became unused to it — he worked only with his pen. It seemed as if fate had

PAUL VON HINTZE

overtaken him. He did not understand how to handle people, and many a misunderstanding arose from this fact. Fortune did not desert him, however. Once more, in 1902, he sat on an office chair — this time in the Admiralty. "I'd like to go to London as naval attaché," he sighed. He had a particular liking for everything English, but his wish was not fulfilled. A year later he was sent to St. Petersburg as marine attaché. Here he laid the foundation of his diplomatic career at the side of the dignified, old Count von Pourtalès. He soon became *persona grata* at the Czar's court, and always had the ear of His Majesty. During the revolution of 1905, when the waves threatened to break over the palace, he ordered a German torpedo boat to Kronstadt and placed it at the service of the Czar in case he should have to flee. His influence continued to increase. He soon became Nicholas II's most faithful adviser. When the revolution seemed to come to no end he advised the Czar to cease trying to appease the masses and take the most rigorous measures against them instead. Hintze's advice was followed and proved good. So much personal influence naturally created enemies among German attachés of the Embassy as well as among the Russians. But enmities and scandals could not shake his position. In 1905 he was frigate Captain; 1906, aide-de-camp to the Kaiser; 1907, Captain; 1908 he was knighted, and in 1909 his title ran as follows:

Military Plenipotentiary at the Imperial Russian Court, attached to the Person of His Majesty, the Czar of all the Russias, and appointed to his Headquarters. One could not get much higher. Peter, as his comrades called him, seemed to have accomplished all there was to accomplish.

Suddenly there was a hitch. Hintze was deposed. The navy lists of 1911 record laconically: Captain Hintze's resignation was accepted in view of his transference to foreign service.

What had happened? A careless remark about "Hessen" had reached ears not meant to hear it. This was Hintze's downfall. The pack were only waiting for it.

When he awoke from the shock he saw that he had tumbled down the stairs. The title of Rear Admiral and the handsome pension that went with it ought to have satisfied Hintze, but the Foreign Office only became a new spring-board for him. He had all sorts of opponents here. They hated the man who was encroaching on their preserves so they packed him off to Mexico, which had so far cost every ambassador his neck. But the Foreign Office had deceived itself; Hintze made possible the impossible, got on a friendly basis with the whole world, easily won everybody's sympathy, and excited great attention by driving his automobile into the midst of a mass of rioters and rescuing a few hard-

PAUL VON HINTZE

pressed Germans. In short, his star of fortune radiated in new splendor. Once more he basked in the sun of the Kaiser's favor. "That's my man!" exclaimed the monarch.

Then came the war. Hintze went to China. Disguised as a stoker he once more crossed the ocean and escaped the persecution of the enemy. "That was finely managed," smiled the Kaiser when Hintze told him of it. "If you do that again I'll make you ambassador to Pekin." After China broke off diplomatic relations he returned home once more. At a critical period he was sent to Christiania as ambassador. He managed very cleverly here also; although unfriendly, Norway remained neutral.

When Mr. Zimmerman had to leave Wilhelmstrasse, Hintze was named as his successor. But he was suspected of being too Pan-German and the Left rejected him. Kühlmann came out winner. After a short stay as Secretary of Foreign Affairs he, too, had to go and Hintze then took his place. He burned most of the Pan-German bridges behind him and made his bow to the Reichstag majority. This splendor did not last long. A few times he spoke publicly: once to the Khedive of Egypt, once to the Irish, and to the Vienna press, whom he assured that there was no suppression of public opinion. He had a friendly word for everyone. It was a heavy defeat for him when Count Burian came out with his offer of peace. Hintze believed he had persuaded the Count from taking this step. He went at last because times were too speedy for his diplomatic methods. He could not imagine a Reichstag plenum. After that he played the rôle of representative of the Foreign Office in the General Headquarters until the crash came.

XXXVII

ROSA LUXEMBURG

The seeds Rosa Luxemburg sowed during her lifetime have begun to sprout. In Berlin on the 10th of January, 1919, machine guns rattled, hand-grenades exploded, and the streets vomited armed proletariat from every corner. These were the days of demonstrations: endless processions with blood-red flags swarmed Unter den Linden, causing the majority socialists and the bourgeois to make counter demonstrations. A gentleman remarked to me in the Chancellor's palace: "Who knows if we will ever see each other alive again?" The days of preparation, of surprises, of dull forebodings, of wild shooting, the days of rioting are over. It has settled down to deadly seriousness. Berlin has become a battle ground, the scene of civil war. The anarchist-communist revolution which aims to weed out capitalism, root and branch, has followed on the heels of the political revolution which sent all the crowned heads of Germany into retirement, and the social revolution of the workers who wished to insure themselves a part of the fruits of the big wage movement. Hegel's philosophical teachings of the pendulum-like movements of development seem to be confirmed. The thesis, Monarchistic absolutism, threatens to be solved by the antithesis, proletariat dictation.

Rosa Luxemburg triumphs. This is her work. For many years she conspired and revolutionized. She did not come from Russian Poland for nothing — not to have learned something of the art of undermining in the political school. About twenty-five years ago she emigrated to Germany after having founded a revolutionary labor party in Poland. Here in Germany she found a new and promising field. But as a foreigner, as a Russian Jewess, she would probably have been quickly deported in Bülow's time if she had not found some quick means of becoming a citizen. She soon found this way in a marriage with a Mr. Lübeck, of whom no one has ever heard since. As Mrs. Rosalie Lübeck she became a Prussian citizen without further parley. She could no longer be deported as a "troublesome foreigner."

But Rosa had sharp thorns; the party felt them more than once. She was clever as was no other Socialist. Was she a woman who had only the feminist movement at heart? Not a bit of it. She was a man who had no time for petty questions, sentimentality, or the like. She went in for the whole thing, always in the front row. She did not clear her path with a dainty parasol after diving up out of the Ghetto — she smashed her way through with a bludgeon. The whole party, even at the time when Bebel and Singer had command, had no small respect for this resolute person. She was a person who commanded respect. And how she could talk! Her words fell like shrapnel on the enemy. She was materialized radicalism working with every rhetorical means at hand. I still remember how she shone resplendent at every party day — how she ironically answered the softer Scheidemann on a day at Jena: *"Du gleichst dem Geist den Du begreifst, nicht mir."* (You resemble the spirit you attack, not me) Everybody shook with laughter. Here the stately, blonde Philip Scheidemann, there the little, undersized, black Rosa with the limping gait.

There was no end to the hubbub she made. She stayed nowhere for any length of time, for she was always raging, always speaking in superlatives, without being able to suggest a better socialistic solution. She stayed but a few years on the *Leipziger Zeitung,* this high school of proletarianism, and for some time she was Karl Kautsky's coworker on the *Neue Zeit.*

Here she scattered her ideas on the tender meadows of science, and during all the years of her development she remained in close touch with Russian Nihilists and Social Revolutionists. Once she was caught by the Russian police and shipped back to Germany, but that did not break off her connections.

LEADERS OF YESTERDAY AND TO-DAY

Some things she had in common with Louise Michel, the great anarchist of the Paris Commune: wild, inflammatory agitation, suggestive fanaticism, and the effect on the masses when she talked to them with her whole soul. When the war broke out she saw the time had come for the solution of her life's work. With Liebknecht, Mehring, and Klara Zetkin, she formed a conspiracy quartet in August or September of 1914. About this time she published her first war pamphlet: *The World Vomits Blood!*

She kept sliding ever farther toward the Left. The greater the war intoxication the more her revolutionary spirit waxed. Gradually this quartet grew to a league in the spring of 1916, which adopted the name of Spartacus. This was at the time when the Social Democratic party split up in dreadful convulsions. She distributed secret circulars and open letters to the labor unions until a certain authority had her arrested and brought to the Breslau prison. Shortly before the 9th of November she and Karl Liebknecht were set at liberty at the order of Scheidemann.

She was loose again. All the resentment she had stored up spiritually and mentally during her years of imprisonment now exploded. In the first November revolution she stood in the front row on the ramparts. But on the second day she saw that this was not *her* revolution. She was still in communication with the

ROSA LUXEMBURG

Independents, at least with Ledebour, Adolph Hoffmann, Eichhorn, Däumig, and Richard Müller, but her heart drew her to Liebknecht, to the people on the extreme left who would hear of no concessions, who wanted to extirpate the bourgeoisie and capitalism, and hand in hand with the Russian Bolshevists spread the world revolution. Ebert's and Haase's revolution seemed but a harmless, capitalist-friendly revolution in dressing gown and slippers, so she went forth and together with Liebknecht founded the *Rote Fahne* (red flag), which whipped up the people day after day with its bloodthirsty fanaticism. She rejected everything: the Erfurt Social Democratic program, parliamentarism, the mining propositions, democracy, everything upon which the Marx socialism was based, and announced at the Berlin conference that the Spartacists were separated from the Independents at last. They could now join the Communists and overthrow the Ebert-Scheidemann Government. "We must be prepared for a period of conflict," she said. "We must undermine the Government by a revolution of the masses."

And that is how it happened that for a week civil war raged in Berlin. The Government recruited more and more troops; narrower and narrower became the circle around the Spartacists. One fort after another fell. Ledebour was arrested. Liebknecht ran into the soldier's net and his faithful Rosa was arrested, too.

LEADERS OF YESTERDAY AND TO-DAY

When she left the exclusive Hotel Eden by the zoölogical gardens, the mob fell upon her in fury with canes and parasols.

She was brutally murdered by the officers who had her in charge, not by the mob. She was struck in the head with the butt end of a gun and afterwards thrown into an automobile and shot. The body was then wrapped with barbed wire and thrown into a canal, where it was not found for weeks. Of the four officers concerned only one was condemned to a year or so of imprisonment, not for the murder of Liebknecht or Rosa Luxemburg, but for some military misdemeanor. He was allowed to escape to Holland on a falsified pass. The trial proceedings may be read in most Berlin papers of that time.

XXXVIII

MAXIMILIAN VON BADEN

This analysis is not easy. In our psychological seminary we have already undertaken a number of psychic dissections, not without success. This case is neither pathologically nor in any other sense abnormal; it is thoroughly commonplace in all its details. Only as a complexity is it difficult to disentangle.

The Prince is in his fifty-second year and has almost thirty years of military service behind him. He was promoted from Lieutenant of the Garde-Kürassier regiment to Lieutenant-General and General of the cavalry. In the first few weeks of the war he was with the fourteenth army corps sent to the defense of Alsace, but "his other duties made it impossible for him to retain this post for any length of time," as his official release reads. So he had only a tiny taste of war and has been but a passive observer. As a militarist he was not prominent; he was one of Nature's chosen ones whose progress could not be stopped by a blue envelope. It was preordained that he should end as General of the cavalry and Excellence. Comradeship and sport fascinated him more than military drill or the routine of barrack life. This was his field; moreover he was not ascetic, he knew how to live like a gentleman. There was nothing to distinguish him from the average either as Prince, officer, or sportsman. Live and let live — shimmering superficiality.

Before the Prince took up a military career he studied law and political science at Freiburg and Heidelberg and took his degree at the University of Leipzig. As officer he read what everybody else read and dipped a little into philosophy, especially Plato and Kant. Plato teaches that it is not the transient and changing life of the senses that is good, but the striving after truth, after an ideal existence. We must refine the soul, free it from everything material in order to become God-like. Applied to the State, this means sacrificing the individual for the benefit of the whole.

To turn from Plato to Christianity: the Prince is religious, Protestant, but not dogmatic. There is something of the genuine pietist in him, something of Spener, Anton, Francke, of Christian mysticism, which seeks to feel, not reason,— which strives for life, not for the purely contemplative.

From the very beginning of the war the Prince took over the care of German prisoners abroad; this was probably the outlet for the craving to help and give advice where everybody was fighting and suffering. He went to work energetically, made frequent trips to

Stockholm and Switzerland, and really accomplished the relief of prisoners in Russia and the removal of interned Germans from France to Switzerland. Whenever exchanged German prisoners crossed the border at Lake Constance, he was there to welcome them home. This was applied Christianity. Kant, too, taught the same thing in his little booklet: *Religion Within the Borders of Reason.* Religion to him meant recognizing one's duties as commandments from God.

The Prince made an ethical-political-religious confession on the 14th of December, 1917, when he became president of the Baden House of Representatives. He examined into the moral foundations of the war with strong, manly words. Although he contested the right of the president of the United States to set himself up as the judge of the world and make war in the name of humanity, he admitted: "We must not deceive ourselves, the American people really believe that the war must continue in order to make the world safe for all the great ideals. It is a tragical fact of this world war that Europe is historically, psychologically, and politically an undiscovered land for the broad masses in America."

After he had designated the democratic parole in the mouths of the Western powers as a "monstrous lie," he raked the Germans over the coals and preached a return from the brutalities of war: "Even in war love for the enemy is the symbol of those who are most faithful to Germany," and " If the world is to become reconciled to the greatness of our power, it must feel that there is a world conscience behind it."

This speech created a great stir at home and abroad. The Kaiser telegraphed the orator calling his speech a deed. Prince Alexander von Hohenlohe, his cousin, the pacifist, wrote him an enthusiastic letter from Switzerland. Max was surprised; the loud applause from the Socialist press was painful to him. " The *Frankfurter Zeitung* should let me alone, and the pacifists too. I am not an ideologist." In the first excitement over the, to him, unpleasant echo, he sat down and wrote a long letter to Prince Alexander:

" In their suggested insanity these newspapers cannot take a word of reason, of serious, practical Christianity for what it is worth. They must first drag it through the mud of their own distortive foolishness in order to fit it to their lower instincts and opinions." The courtier speaks from the letter, the blue-blood who will have his Christianity for himself, who feels himself compromised and embarrassed by the applause from the other bank of the river, and shakes it off with a shudder. In order that the others may not imagine he belongs to them — to the democrats in slouch hats and dirty fingernails — he adds: " Naturally I wish the greatest possible exploitation of our success and in contrast to the peace resolutions, which are the child of fear and Berlin dog-days, I wish as much compensation possible so that we may not be too poor after the war." This letter, written in a bad humor by one who was ashamed of the confessions of his own soul, was written confidentially and for a long time the public knew nothing of it.

The Prince, who had been the subject of conversation for a few weeks, again passed into the background of silence. He lived with his thoughts and often listened to the words of Dr. Johannes Müller, who had great influence over him: Johannes Müller, the man who knitted up the raveled sleeve of care, who traveled about in winter giving lectures and in summer, in Emmau by Patenkirchen, conducted a soul-sanatorium. Here come soul-tired, seeking people who live during the day as in any other pension; at night they are spiritually refreshed by Dr. Müller. He is no dogmatic, mechanical, theologian; he wrestles with his God. When he lectures or writes for his scattered parish he lets a plumb line down into the soul, deeper and deeper, listening and feeling what is stored away down there untouched by the material. He spins his listeners into a web of finest thought sensations, and only he who is equipped cap-a-pie with critical reason can withstand the murmuring melodies of his ethics which often become blurred, muddled, and foolish when brought down from the spiritual heights onto the flatlands of practical life. But no one goes away empty-handed. He has something to say to each. Even the Prince has more than once gone away with rich food for thought.

On August 22, 1918, in a general meeting held by both Houses of the Baden Landtag to celebrate the centennial of their constitution, Prince Max made a speech. This time somewhat formal, but the ethical seeped through even here. "The danger of a moral-national illness threatens us," he said, "but it can be exorcised if our spiritual leaders remain conscious of their duties as the guards and healers of the people's souls." He then acknowledged his faith in a League of Nations.

We have still to examine the milieu in which he grew to manhood. Much was anticipated. His father was Prince Wilhelm of Baden, the eldest of the two brothers of the Grand Duke, Friedrich I. His mother, Princess Marie, can trace her ancestry to Napoleon's time. She was a Duchess of Leuchtenberg and a granddaughter of Eugen Beauharnais, who was Napoleon I's stepson and vice-regent of Italy. Prince Max is married to Princess Marie of Cumberland, the oldest sister of Duke Ernst August of Braunschweig. His connections on both sides are splendid. He played no small part in the reconciliation of the Hohenzollerns and the Guelphs. From his international connections and also from his friendship with the Social Democrat,

MAXIMILIAN VON BADEN

Ludwig Frank, we get a new glimpse of his humanitarian cosmopolitanism which rises above mere nationalism to the plane of common humanity.

In October when Count Hertling resolved to resign from the chancellorship in order to make room for the new régime, Herr von Berg, chief of the imperial cabinet, suggested Prince Max as his successor. Fehrenbach, president of the Reichstag, and von Payer, Vice-Chancellor, had refused the position. The Prince came, saw, and conquered. His good reputation preceded him. People said he had warned them at Headquarters against a spring offensive, but they had not listened to him. The Prince got into touch with the party leaders and soon agreed with them; the way was cleared over night for a parliamentary system. Progressives, Center, and Social Democrats were called into the cabinet. The conservatives were also invited. At the request of the army leaders his first act was to send a message to Wilson asking for truce and peace transactions. His clear, open speech in the Reichstag, in which he plainly announced the beginning of a new period, pleased everybody immensely. Only the conservatives were horrified at this princely leader of the people's Government.

And then — through some indiscretion of the Paris press, that unfortunate letter to Prince von Hohenlohe was made public. There was a hasty vote. The Prince declared his loyalty. The parties discussed the matter and concluded to overlook the purely human impulse. Even the Social Democrats forgave him; there were larger things at stake — for instance, peace. In this way under her Princely Chancellor, Germany was thoroughly democratized. Militarism was rooted out, stock and branch, and the imperial power was vested in the Civil Government. These reforms went through in quick time, but it was all over in less than six weeks. Even the Prince had to step aside for the revolution.

Was he a great politician? Hardly, but at least he was not of the old Bismarck school. The time for diplomatic tricks, for countermoves, was over. Germany marched headlong into the world catastrophe from this sort of politics. The Prince wanted to see what candid honesty would do, trusting in the conscience of the world.

But before his plea for truce was answered he had to make way for the Socialist, Ebert.

XXXIX

KURT EISNER

When the Royal orchestra, under Weingartner's leadership, gave its symphony concerts, a little man gladly climbed four long flights of stairs to the gallery, where there was standing room only, to listen to the sweet strains of music. This was Kurt Eisner, modest, unpretentious, silent — introspective journalist and politician. A Social Democrat at a time when it was not fashionable to speak of such things. A votary, but not one to hold beery speeches with pathetic gestures in a smoky beer hall. His fine feeling prevented this; he was no people's politician. He wrote splendidly, intelligently, and sarcastically, and yet not for the nameless masses. At the end of the old century, when he accepted Wilhelm Liebknecht's call to the *Vorwärts,* he was the one editor in Berlin who dazzled most without being himself a dazzler.

He came from a simple Berlin home and began as a Democrat. He studied philosophy and Germanism for eight semesters and then looked about for some way to earn his bread. His first books, *Psychopathia Spiritualis* and *Friedrich Nietzsche,* brought him neither fame nor money. At the age of twenty-five he began to write for the press — for the *Frankfurter Zeitung* — and then for the *Landeszeitung* in Marburg. Here the Jew came into conflict with anti-Semitism. In the stormy election days of that time one of his circulars attracted especial attention. "How is it, you farmers of Hessen," he wrote, "how is it that you do not know that your candidate, Böckel, has sixteen illegitimate children? Is it to such a person that you want to give your vote?" But Kurt Eisner did not know these lusty farmers. Never did Böckel receive so many votes as then; the sixteen illegitimate children had suddenly endeared him to the people.

From Marburg Eisner's writings found their way into the rest of the world roundabout. His article: "A Political New Year's Reception," got him a month in jail. The court considered it an insult to His Majesty. In August, 1898, when he had served his time, the *Vorwärts* received him into the fold again. He threw his whole soul into political life; his severity knew no bounds. With splendid bravery he led the battle against the new high tariffs. I still remember his biting article entitled, "Tax-crazy," and the night he devoted to the Reichstag when the Left wing tried to obstruct the passage of the bill by long speeches. Antrick (Social Democrat) alone spoke eight hours. The afternoon passed by, it became evening, night, midnight, and still he spoke on. It was Saturday; the long-coated Center people wanted to go home in order not to leave their flocks without a shepherd over Sunday. They stood around stamping their feet and swinging their hand bags in impatience. They could not leave until the fateful vote was taken. *"Heute geht Herrendienst vor Gottesdienst"* (Representative service comes before church service to-day. Literally: Lord's service comes before God's service), wrote Eisner dryly. The obstruction was finally broken; the Junkers, factory barons, Conservatives, Center, and National Liberals won out. And I remember how he turned the Conservative socialist-eaters' own words against them: "Nothing is holy to such beings, not even the majesty of the people."

His ideas were inexhaustible; he was never embarrassed for words. He listened to everything without insolence, and then coolly and clearly gave back his reflections. An introspective man he was, sufficient unto himself, a Sybarite in a cold, carpetless room, a radical who did not intoxicate himself with words, but a man of careful thought who gave from his inmost soul. He was shy, hesitating, and modest as a young maiden who blushes at a word. Moreover, he was not really radical at that time; he was a revisionist like Eduard Bernstein, whom he resembled in many other ways. At the Dresden party days in 1903, when the dirty party clothes were being thoroughly washed — when one bad odor after another polluted the atmosphere — when Bebel, with fire and sword, sought to stamp out revisionism — the verdict against the *Vorwärts* was also brought in. The "noble six" were kicked out. Kurt Eisner stuck to the reviled ones and so the whole editorial staff flew. With a shout of triumph Däumig and company, Stadthagen and Adolph Hoffman took over the *Vorwärts* and steered her course bravely onto the stormy high seas of radicalism. Kurt Eisner was again out in the cold; would he have to begin all over again? Once when his pocket book was always empty he had been happy when some Philistine paper accepted his articles, or when he could get a bit of hack-work to do such as a congress report. Were these hand-to-mouth days to begin all over again? The articles he had already published brought him in no money at all. These were "The Junker Revolt"; "Wilhelm Liebknecht"; "Spirit of the Day"; "The Future State of To-day", and "Königsberg, the Czar's Secret Compact". For a few years he lived precariously. Finally, in 1907, the socialistic *Fränkische Tagespost* in Nürnberg engaged him as editor-in-chief. He became a naturalized Bavarian in order to be able to accomplish more politically. Again his publications made him known far beyond the outskirts of the old Dürer city. Not as representative or party delegate, which he never was at any time during his life. He spoke very badly at this time — was anything but a public speaker, so that the party could use him only as a reporter.

But those precarious years following his dismissal from the *Vorwärts* had one advantage — during this time he made a study of foreign politics. The first fruits of these studies was his booklet on Morocco, *The Sultan of the World War,* which announced the approaching catastrophe.

Nürnberg held him fast for three years, then he moved to Munich where he published the *Arbeiter Feuilleton,* which was used by almost the whole democratic press, and became coworker on the *Münchener Post*. On many a discussion evening he sought to enlighten the working masses. In this way he gradually learned to talk.

And then the war broke out. As correspondent of the *Chemnitzer Volksstimme* — Noske's paper — he brought out the first announcements in regard to the now unavoidable catastrophe — the result of Russian war policy, as he then believed. The revisionist gradually became a radical — like Bernstein. Everything he wrote was confiscated by the censor, so he soon confined himself to dramatic criticism. He saw the misfortune approaching ever nearer and nearer, and attempted to stave it off, to hold it back. The workers should arise and put an end to this wholesale butchery: " every wheel stands still, if only your strong arm wills." He had long ago joined the Independents. In February, 1918, the time seemed ripe. He helped to fan the flames of the general strike movement in Munich. Together with Frau Eugen Lersch, he was arrested on the night of February 1st and put in prison, where he remained for eight and one-half months. Shut off from the world without the possibility of helping to hasten the coming revolution, he wrote and wrote, and finally concluded a new series, *The Dreams of a Prophet.*

On a September day the doors of his prison opened. The party had put him up for the Reichstag in place of Georg von Vollmar, who wished to retire from political life. A few weeks afterwards the revolutionary waves from Kiel began to ripple. Eisner's great moment had come.

Enormous gatherings and huge demonstration parades everywhere, Munich included. Berlin was quiet; they did not yet hear the roar of the tidal wave. It had just begun to whisper. But the waves were already roaring in Munich. On the sixth of November they broke loose. But we will let Eisner himself speak: "Two days before the revolution, when the masses gathered on the Theresien meadow, when this thousand-headed throng began to call for deeds and to threaten to march that very night into Munich to begin the revolution, I cried out to them: 'I will wager my head that

KURT EISNER

in forty-eight hours all Munich will arise.' This promise was kept almost to the minute. If I had said that same morning that the reign of the Wittelsbachs, who had ruled for eight hundred years, would be over within a few hours — that a Bavarian Republic would be proclaimed — they would have locked me in an insane asylum."

Instead of the insane asylum he marched into the ministerial palace at the head of laborers, soldiers, and scholars — overthrew the old powers, the court and all its parasites, bureaucracy, and the whole crumbling, degenerated system. He then constituted the councils of Workmen, Soldiers, and Farmers, took over the management, and during the night of the 8th of November issued the first proclamation: "Bavaria's socialistic civil war is ended. The working masses will be united on the basis of our revolutionary program. Long live the Bavarian Republic! Long live peace! Long live the work of all Workers!" Other proclamations followed, speeches, revolutionary poems, political utterances — all esthetic enjoyments.

Kurt Eisner, whose life was spent in toil and trouble, grew old before his time. A gray, shaggy beard framed his face. Deep furrows lined his restless brow. His large, noble forehead seemed larger because of an almost bald head. Behind, the hair fell on his shabby coat like that of a patriarch. His shoulders are bent. A heavy nickel-framed pince-nez rested on a broad nose. His eyes had red, tired lids, but his mind was fresh and active. Kurt Eisner, Bavarian minister-president, was suddenly spoken of the world over.

The old democracy, the old partiamentary system was broken, he said. New forms must be created and he would create them. The Workers, Soldiers, and Farmers' Councils would be the fundamental principle. He seemed to wish to return to a medieval system based on professions, but hesitated and kept his promise to stand for a National Assembly. The press he knew so well made him uncomfortable — he reflected upon some means to extract the poison from its fangs but was dismayed at the idea of repressing public opinion. He would have liked to banish all those guilty of the war, to proscribe those who worked for it afterwards—Scheidemann, David, Solf, and Erzberger. Rather should Bavaria conclude a separate peace than sit at the table with such compromised politicians. When Berlin did not react to this he sent an ultimatum threatening to break off all relations with the Foreign Office. Berlin laughed, called him a charlatan, a fool, a carnival joke come to life; he could write beautifully but it was impossible for him to think or act politically.

Was Berlin right I wonder? Eisner saw in Germany the only guilty party in the war; he probed in the wounds of his nation.

KURT EISNER

The despotic politicians on the other side of the Rhine laughed at him as an ideologist, intoxicated by beautiful, sweeping, painful gestures.

Eisner's attitude caused considerable excitement in Munich and created an atmosphere charged with electricity. An explosion might follow at any moment. When Eisner, under the pressure of the Bourgeois element and the Majority Social Democrats, finally decided to call together the Bavarian Constituent Assembly, the Communists had determined to make its opening session the signal for giving battle. Just then a strange thing happened. The Reactionaries took a hand in the action. On February 21, 1919, Eisner, while on his way to the session of the Parliament, was shot down by a young, rattle-brained Nationalist, Count Arco-Valley, and only half an hour later the Communists forced their way into the Diet and at the very moment when a eulogy in honor of the assassinated Eisner was to be pronounced began to fire on the ministers. The Social Democratic minister Auer was severely wounded by a revolver shot, an officer and a delegate were killed. The Bavarian Soviet Republic was now proclaimed and the dark days of Munich's Red Terror were ushered in.

XL

WILHELM KARL DITTMANN

Whenever I see Dittmann I am reminded of Hjalmar Ekdal in Ibsen's *Wild Duck*. He is an imposing, impressive man — tall, slender, with a beautiful mane of light brown hair, a pointed beard, and a jaunty mustache above it. Two keen eyes that one does not soon forget. But there is something about him that makes him a bit ridiculous — a discrepancy somewhere between will and ability, between what he really is and what he seems to be. Like the difference between an artist and his photograph, between a scholar and the druggist clerk with his "highfalutin'" plans while mixing pills and salve.

Hjalmar had a liking for grand sounding words which always contradicted his actions. Gregers Werle compares the Ekdals to the picture of a wild duck: "Diving under, she bit into the seaweed and became so entangled that she could not come up again unless some dog could bring her up, even against her will."

Dittmann bit into radicalism so firmly that he could not come up again although he longed to be on top. He, too, awaited a Gregers Werle to pull him out. He was drawn into the revolutionary cabinet as a lusty Independent; daily placed before new and practical decisions, he had to act, to show his colors. All at once he saw that nothing was ever accomplished by mere criticism or pathos — that one did not get very far with Ledebour passion, which was ready to demolish everything at once, but that actions also meant responsibility. In these few weeks of governing he began to slide more and more toward the Right and began to approach Ebert, Scheidemann, and Landsberg, the once reviled Social Democrats.

At the congress of councils, when Ledebour's poisonous arrows prickled, he made a confession of faith in common socialism which unites both sides in spite of momentary problems or tactics. He admonished his comrades to unite for the National Assembly election, to present a united front to the enemy, capitalism, and insure the safety of the fruits of the revolution. He saw his Gregers Werle in the masses, who would act in this manner whether the leader will or no. The leader must be the tool of the masses. The radicals, all the big and little Ledebours, trembled with disgust and rage at this recalcitrant who had suddenly deserted his colors.

In the last act Hjalmar Ekdal, with a pathetic gesture, is about to leave his wife, Gina, from whose past Gregers Werle lifted the veil. He packs his things, gathers up all the odds and ends, and is already pulling on his overcoat when Gina all of a sudden places bread, butter, meat and beer on the table. Hjalmar sees it, sniffs a few times and decides to remain — at least for a moment. He stays for good.

Dittmann was one of the most savage in the battle against the backsliding majority Socialists — he began to rampage with hands and feet if he only smelled them from a distance. Then they placed a dish of meat before him in the shape of a seat in the cabinet, and he, too, decided to remain — for a time. His place in the Government grew cosier and for a few weeks he left the radicalism to his companions outside.

From the very beginning he had served Social Democracy. He was born at Eutin, 1874, on a dull November day. There he attended the people's school and for four years learned the joiner's trade. He had a firm fist, went at a job energetically, and soon made the chips fly. The Philistines got goose-flesh when he began to stir up the proletariat against capitalism. At the age of twenty-one he became member of the party and the Trade Union, and wandered through almost the whole of Schleswig-Holstein, Mecklenburg, province Brandenburg, and finally settled in Berlin. Here he worshiped the Great Ones from afar and was initiated into the higher mysteries of socialism. In 1899 he was sent to Bremenshaven as editor of the *Norddeutsche Volksstimme*. The way to fame and success lay straight be-

WILHELM KARL DITTMAN

fore him. Three years later he was sent in the same capacity to Solingen and was called from there to Frankfurt am Main as party secretary. He was the first Social Democrat to enter the city council. The gods regarded him with favor, *i. e.,* the party gods. For he spoke with a beautiful, sonorous voice, made an impression on the lovely bevy of lady cashiers, and when he unleashed his anger against the capitalistic world — when he pretended to have the key to the realization of Marx's dogma (Hjalmar's secret discovery) then his listeners would jump from their seats and applaud until the walls trembled. With fluttering necktie and waving mane he could bow gratefully while the young ladies of the party, their modest bosoms decorated with red ribbons, whispered in each others' ears: "Isn't he just grand! Just like the moving picture hero!"

In 1909 he was again editor in Solingen. He had to do penance for many an impulsive word written and spoken. As party delegate he was sent to Bremen, Leipzig, Magdeburg, and Jena, and also took part in the International Socialistic Congress at Stuttgart and at Copenhagen. It was rather late when he entered the Reichstag in 1912. Here he settled down at the extreme left wing and was not to be joked with. In spite of this, he approved of the war credit and participated in the policy of August, 1914, until he was at last initiated to a higher knowledge and, together with Ledebour and Haase, separated himself from the Scheidemann people — his bosom friends of yesterday. They opened up a firm of their own — the Labor party, from which sprung the Independent Social Democrats. He reached the height of his parliamentary accomplishments during the prison debate when he carried almost the whole House with him with his well-tempered pathos. Behind the scenes he was not backward in preparing the way for the revolution. He was also mixed up in the mutiny of 1917, but came off with a black eye. The next time he was not so fortunate — during the January strike in Berlin, when he was really trying to pour oil on the troubled waves, he was arrested while making a speech to the demonstrating masses, and put behind the bars.

The 9th of November brought him freedom as it did many others. After that he sat in high council with the people's representatives and helped to decide Germany's fate. But only for a month and a half. After the bloody Christmas day before the palace he resigned from the cabinet, together with his "Independent" comrades, because the people on the street demanded it and because one cannot govern long with two souls in one's breast.

XLI

ADOLPH GROEBER

A Württemberg Democrat of the old stock, for when he speaks he does not conceal his thoughts, he fires away like a booming cannon. A long, grizzled white beard and bushy mane of hair frame his ruddy countenance. A pair of spectacles that sit astride the middle of his nose, and a slightly bent figure lend Adolph Groeber a sort of comfortable atmosphere; Santa Claus of the Center, St. Nicholas with his sack full of political toys. His father used to be a manufacturer of toys somewhere down in Riedlingen. He, the son, has transformed the same material into intellect and now plays with politics. Tin soldier or politician — both are shoved around by the rough hands of fate and placed upright again when they tumble down.

Groeber got to know the alternating political game better than most. He entered the Reichstag in 1887, when Bismarck drove the anti-militarists, Windhorst, Richter, and Grillenberger, into a combine, when he dissolved Parliament and forged the cartel of Conservatives and National Liberals. In these turbulent times, when other Center men were beaten, he came off victor and was elected. Two years later he was sent to the Württemberg Landtag. As a faithful Eckart of Catholic democracy, he took an active part in all the quickly changing political phases of that time. He spread his wide coat protectively over the Poles and the labor representatives whenever the feudal wing of the Conservatives — the Junkers and Agrarians — lifted up their heads too impudently. He was a zealous partisan of social politics, and regarded the Catholic Church and her political gate-keepers, the Center party in Germany, as something above the State — as international. The teachings of the Holy One were meant for all the world, for the Latin, as well as the Germanic and the Slav peoples. Even the negroes were not excluded. They were all human beings to him — human beings who thirsted after the salvation of their souls. God loved them all equally well — Jesus and Mother Mary, too. Only the saints seemed to be somewhat partial. For instance, Cyrill and Methodius had their preference for the Poles, Czechs and Bulgarians; Adelbertus for the Lithuanians, and St. Joseph . . . Oh, well, you know all the little weaknesses.

I still remember about ten years ago how friend Matthias Erzberger spoke in the Reichstag on the immortality of the negro's soul. Carried away by his own pathos, he almost lost himself in the Elysian regions of the black man's paradise. It was a long-winded affair and the tired heads of the assembly soon began to nod so devoutly one might think sleep was about to overtake them. At this juncture, when one could almost hear the seconds ticking past, someone on the tribune laughed aloud. Disturbed in his religious thoughts, Groeber flung a curse at the journalists' bench: "These journalists, these swine!" That was a poke in a wasp's nest. The journalists were indignant and struck. They went to the president of the House and negotiations began. The president wouldn't apologize and Groeber wouldn't. There was a session going on, but the world never knew anything of it. Even the *Reichsanzeiger* struck with the following comment: "On account of certain proceedings in the Reichstag session of March 19, 1908, the press representatives have laid down their work for an indefinite period. Therefore, this account contains only the resolutions brought up at the session and the declaration of the Bundesrat table." The strike was sanctioned by the Government. Prince Bülow, who was to make his great speech, kept putting if off and finally contrived to bring about a compromise. Mr. Groeber apologized and the meeting went on.

Groeber's position in the party was not affected in the least by this little episode. He continued to oppose the Conservatives and his power kept on the increase. He was the third after Hertling and Spahn. When Hertling was called to the Bavarian cabinet, Spahn became Minister of Justice, and Fehrenbach president of the Reichstag, then Groeber became first. He and Erzberger set the pace for the party — Groeber, the elder, holding the check-rein, Erzberger, the younger, ever pushing forward. Groeber with his belief in political authority, Erzberger without respect for tradition; Groeber, champion of a League of Nations from a Catholic viewpoint, and of universal disarmament, Erzberger his tractable pupil. Groeber was the party specialist on all international questions.

No wonder he had gone through the usual juristic routine — from barrister in Rottweil to director of the provincial court in Heilbronn. With years came also the burdens of political offices. He entered the executive committee of the Center party, this Folks Verein for Catholic Germany, and presided frequently on great days. At last he was leader of the Center faction in the Reichstag and, after von Payer, leader of the interfactional committee of the Reichstag majority parties. After having neither supported nor helped to overthrow the Chancellor, Count Hertling, he became Secretary of State without a portfolio, in the new parliamentary Government. With von Payer and Scheidemann he formed the trifolium about the new Prince Chancellor. They who had been sitting in the critics' parquet were now active players on the political stage.

And people had already numbered him among the

ADOLPH GROEBER

"has-beens"! It was not so long ago that he was seriously ill and sent for the priest to administer the last sacrament before his expected departure for another world. He is already sixty-five years old and his burdens have grown heavier with the years.

When he passes through the corridors of the Reichstag he is generally encased in two or three black coats buttoned up to the neck. In Berlin he lives in a modest Christian hospice, and every morning he takes his little airing in the Tiergarten. In winter when the snow covers the earth and he goes stamping through the drifts, the children stand still and ask if that really is Santa Claus. . . .

XLII

EMIL EICHHORN

I knew them all — the Berries, Stubenrauch, Jagow, and Oppen — who held the rascals of Berlin in check during the last ten or twelve years with an army of bluecoats. They were not mere police presidents, like their colleagues in more prominent cities — they were more, they were Governors to a greater or less degree according to their standing, and the strongest supports of the old secular system that was centralized in Berlin. Direct telephone connections with the palace, with all Imperial official buildings and the Ministry excluded all chance of surprise. A little pressure on a button, a flash of light in the telephone central, and the thousand-windowed fortress on Alexanderplatz immediately vomited forth an army on foot, on horse, and in civilian, ready to dash in wherever there promised to be trouble.

In this Alexander castle the president was enthroned, in rooms 162–63. The presidents are all immortalized by portraits on the walls of the reception room, like pastors who have left their flocks for more blissful regions. Nineteen portraits already hang here. The first, a lithograph of President Gruner, who heads the list in 1809, is badly faded. Herr von Oppen, who had to flee before the masses as they poured into these sacred rooms during the November revolution, did not have time to dedicate his portrait to the ancestral hall. Herr Eichhorn, the great revolutionary president, had still less time, and, if I know the gentleman well, it will probably not be missed. His name will live in documents, but he will not be placed on show.

When I first saw him in all his new dignity, it was at a conference where he was busy expounding new ideas. A haggard, slender man, already past fifty, yellowish complexion, prominent cheek-bones, long, greasy hair carefully brushed back from his forehead, a skimpy, bluish-green mustache on the ends. Heavens! he looked harmless enough, simple, modest, and prudent, a regular Philistine.

As he unrolled his program, how good it sounded — so full of insight, charity, and fairness! Surely things will be different now! "But you must give me time. It can't be done all at once. The policemen shall henceforth be called Safety men. The weapons which have caused so much bad blood among the public shall be taken away from them. And then prostitution shall be regulated in a different manner; the criminal police system shall be reorganized. And then of course you want to know what my political convictions are. I am a political officer. I am socialistic, on the left side — Independent. The interests of the people are the most important thing to me. My greatest desire is that the people of Berlin shall have confidence in me. Oh, yes — they talk of the Bolshevists over there in Russia with so much disgust. Of course I am no Bolshevist, but the people should not let themselves be so easily fooled. The Bolshevists are not as black as they are painted. Most reports are exaggerated. And the papers — yes — I say it merely to show that even if one is not a Bolshevist one must be fair to one's opponent. And, as I said before, the police are to be disarmed. Then the public will have confidence in me."

Heavens, I thought, Social Democracy did not pitch out a mental giant, exactly, for the head of their police system. I quite comprehend that the majority Socialist, Eugen Ernst, would have been preferable. But Eichhorn had the strongest elbows and pushed his way to the front an hour earlier. In order to keep on good terms with the Independents in the Government they made the best of the situation. The chief of the chancellery, a dignified gentlemen who has already served six or seven masters, told me half-confidentially that Mr. Eichhorn was always very pleasant and obliging, but . . .

But what? Well, one must not know his political past. He was a genuine, easy-going Saxon, born in Röhrsdorf by Chemnitz, Germany's political storm pot. Once Johannes Most, the savage anarchist and communist, triumphed there. About thirty years ago

EMIL EICHHORN

he wrote: "Give us a thousand wheelwrights and in three months the revolution will be there: poison and daggers, dynamite and nitroglycerin, revolvers and torches, shall lay waste the world . . ."

Eichhorn had nothing in common with Most's hot-blooded temperament; he was brought up on slops and butter bread. He attended the public school and later private technical institutes, but he did not have to hide his light under a bushel — its flame was scarcely visible as it was. Finally he became — Oh, ye Gods and nine Muses — a glacier. When he entered the Labor Union movement he broke a good many party windows. In spite of his easy-going Saxon disposition, it was very soon discovered that he was radical — super-radical. Nevertheless he woke up one day as chairman of the Glaziers' organization, a new organizer was discovered.

But he longed for intellectual fields; the glass-cutter had served its purpose. Glue pot and scissors — these were his ideals henceforth. He became editor in Dresden; now he could shine — you ought to have seen him. This was the way to handle the scissors and dip the brush in the glue pot! This was the way to show the bourgeois what was what. But before he could finish this war on paper he was called to Karlsruhe as secretary of the Workers' party. Here he was mild as butter because the South Germans, and especially the Baden people, were not fond of radicalism.

He climbed high and higher, became editor again in Mannheim, city councillor of the same place, and member of the Baden Landtag. The district of Pforzheim-Durlach sent him to the Reichstag. Now he could show these crazy Philistines a thing or two! But he didn't — he enjoyed himself with slops and butter bread again. Only when he came back from Berlin was he radical once more. Gradually the Badener party got wise to the fact that he was only a blustering noodle-pate, and he was not put up as candidate in 1912. They had had enough of him.

Now he angrily burned all bridges behind him; he left ungrateful Baden and settled in Berlin, where he found a small position in the Social Democrat press bureau. He was Johnny-on-the-spot at the party split-up. New stars beckoned, new successes. He stirred up one mess after another, became a welcome guest of Liebknecht, Rühle, Dittmann, and Ledebour, and kept himself fresh in their minds in case of a decisive change in the party. And right-o — he was appointed chief of the U. S. P. D.'s press bureau. When Herr Joffe, with his Bolshevik staff, took possession of the Russian embassy, Eichhorn and his wife joined the Rosta — that notorious Bolsheviki espionage factory — for the sum of one thousand five hundred marks monthly. Now he had revolutionary ground under his feet and could prepare for that which was to come.

EMIL EICHHORN

At last he stood there as police president of Berlin with, oh, such noble intentions. While the police were being disarmed in order to "win the confidence of the public," he was secretly arming the radical Berlin laborers and gradually turning the police headquarters into an arsenal and a fortress. His Spartacist doings became more and more open and one could count the days on one's fingers until the Red Guard was to be let loose on Berlin. The socialistic Government hesitated, and when they finally removed him from office it was the signal for the counter-revolution from the Left. Eight days Berlin was a battlefield — a struggle between Spartacists and the Government. One barricade after another was taken by the Government troops, and at last the police präsidium surrendered. In the meantime Eichhorn occupied another fortress, the Bötzow brewery; when this was threatened he fled.

Eichhorn is a very questionable figure. He was not a person to fight openly and honestly for his principles. Money — much money stuck to his fingers. He sent many a one to his death who believed he was fighting for political faith. He let loose the scum of Berlin against peaceful citizens; in grotesque inversion he did his best to make Berlin unsafe.

This intellectually insignificant man in the mask of a Philistine is really comical. He can boast of having turned everything topsy-turvy for a few weeks.

XLIII

KARL LIEBKNECHT

Did you see him in that big, automobile truck speaking to the crowd pressing around? Did you see the machine guns on both sides of him? Did you see the gloomy eavesdroppers in the midst of the mass, their hands on the handle of the revolver in their pocket, ready to shed their blood and the blood of others for their hero up there on the wagon? Do you feel the uncanny, suggestive power that Liebknecht pours over the solid mass of people when he speaks? His protruding eyes roll wildly as if to bore the brains of his audience. His hands are constantly in motion; now he tears open his jacket, strikes his chest dramatically and shrieks: "Brothers, comrades, shoot me dead if what I say is not true!" The next moment he runs his fingers through his hair, thrusts out his head and hurls these words at his listeners: "To the lamp-post with Ebert and Scheidemann, the bloodhounds!"

The people become excited — red flags are unfurled, and quickly a line is formed to parade through the center of Berlin.

It is the same old story ever since the revolution has begun to feel at home. The *Rote Fahne* prints these

KARL LIEBKNECHT

Liebknecht and Luxemburg tirades every day. The Berliner used to feel the cold chills running up and down his back when he read them, but he has gradually grown used to them and no longer takes these " counter revolutions " tragically.

Is this slender, little man of forty-seven years merely a demon-ridden fanatic? Or has the border between intellect and madness already been crossed?

Let us look back over his life, perhaps we shall find the key there. Wilhelm, his father, was a revolutionist of '48, and took part in the Baden uprising which was suppressed by Prussian troops. The old man's socialistic principles cost him something; nowhere did he find peace or rest for long. Now he was expelled from this place and now from that. More than once he was imprisoned. One year after Karl's birth he and August Bebel were sentenced to two years in the fortress at Hubertusburg for treason. Between periods of exile and imprisonment he wrote for the newspapers, for the *Norddeutsche Allgemeine Zeitung,* the *Volksstaat,* and finally for the *Vorwärts.* Besides these he wrote a great many socialistic booklets and pamphlets, mostly propagandistic. Bismarck persecuted him with all the energy of his strong personality. At the beginning of the Franco-Prussian war, when the Reichstag brought in the bill for war-credit, Liebknecht and Bebel withheld their votes.

LEADERS OF YESTERDAY AND TO-DAY

The boy Karl never stood very well with his father, who was idolized by the proletariat more than any other party veteran. There was very little in common between them except fanatic conviction and an excessive imagination. The father's imagination, however, did not extend so much to politics — he was always practical. But it was different with Karl. He was very stubborn and not to be influenced by his father. In Leipzig, where he was born, he enjoyed the usual middle class upbringing, attending the grammar school, the Nicolai gymnasium, and then went into "exile" with his father when he was expelled from Leipzig by the socialistic laws. They settled for the time being in the suburb, Borsdorf. Karl took his examinations in Berlin and entered the university there. Even as a student he carried on a reckless social agitation, always belonged to the most radical set, and was a welcome guest at the laborers' assemblies in the north and east of Berlin. Only one thing he lacked, and that was the gift of speech. He spoke very indistinctly, lisped, and had a high, falsetto voice which changed so frequently that his hearers almost smiled with pity. But his iron energy overcame even this. Like Demosthenes, he did not give up until his speech was distinct and clear, although he never acquired the sonorous resonance he would have liked to possess. He longed to speak, and if he displeased the people, he would pour so much passion into his words that they would be compelled to listen to him. And that is what he did.

In Würzburg, where the world at the foot of the proud Marienburg begins to be fascinatingly beautiful, he received his *Doctor Juris et Rerum Politicarum*. Restless and unmannerly, he passed three or four barrister years in Augsburg, Paderborn, and Hamm, always in strict Catholic neighborhoods. Curiously enough, he once related before a public meeting that he was directly descended from Martin Luther on his father's side. After passing the examination for assistant judge he became a lawyer and settled down in Berlin like his brother. His practice increased rapidly, for he was after all the son of a famous father. The proletariat swarmed to him — he gradually became the outcasts' defender. His following in the socialistic forum also increased. Through his reckless radicalism, which knew no bounds even then, he whipped up the masses. He often got a dressing down from old Bebel, who soon broke off all personal relations with him, although he had once been an intimate friend of the father's.

In 1902 Liebknecht obtained his first post of honor; he became city councillor and a member of the Charity Board. Six years, together with a few others, he entered the Prussian House, which up to now had been socialistically pure. Here he fought many a round with the dignified, long-bearded, Count Schwerin-

Löwitz. Like a naughty boy, he strained at the regulations, sought to upset the petrified traditions of the House, and tried to lead a small class-campaign on his own account.

His special hobby was anti-militaristic propaganda, which he carried even into the barracks. His little book, *Militarism and anti-Militarism,* left no doubt as to his opinions. The court interfered, and his forensic dialectic had no effect on the red-robed judges at Leipzig; he was sentenced to one and a half years at the fortress — after all one could not forbid him his fanatic idealism. He was sent to the fortress at Glatz, and here he had time to think over his life and make plans for the future. Between these gloomy and joyless four walls, in the midst of soldiers eternally coming and going, his beliefs became the more firmly fixed. Hate and repulsion for the middle classes, capitalistic and militaristic society, ate deeper and deeper into his soul. More and more compelling became the inner command to break up this bourgeois verein by a revolution of the proletariat. After this test, after the days and nights of brooding, which only strengthened his ideals, he again issued forth into the midst of human society. New impulses drove him to new actions. In 1910 he went to America, as his father had done before him, in order to escape the suffocating, political atmosphere of Germany. Over there, across the great pond, he was likely to become enlightened. He would see capitalism in all its power and monstrous concentration, and see that the German laborer is really far better off than his brother in America.

He published an article to this effect, but his observations did not affect his principles. Soon after his return he again mixed in the whirlpool of radicalism. In 1912 he was sent to the Reichstag from Potsdam-Osthavelland, the Kaiser's district, where he had served in the Garde-Pioneer Battalion. Here he started in with a will. Once when he was planning an attack, he sent a message to the journalists' tribune asking them to speak as well as possible of him. There was a strong strain of vanity in him. The speech was against Krupp and the ammunition factories, against some dark bribery stories, and against the international combination of the Krupp, Ehrhard, Creusot, Armstrong, and all the other ammunition capitalists. Great was the attention his revelations attracted at home and abroad. For days Liebknecht was the center of discussion. Conceit began to fan his soul; he began to strive toward an unattainable goal. When the Russian Czar was about to come to Germany to visit his grand ducal brother-in-law, Liebknecht screamed to a Magdeburg gathering: "Germany should show this bloody Czar the door!" A new rumpus! The diplomats calmed the Russians and Liebknecht was held for trial.

LEADERS OF YESTERDAY AND TO-DAY

And then came the war. When it started Liebknecht did not leave the assembly room as did Representative Kunert, when the first milliard credit was being voted for. Bethmann-Hollweg announced in a loud voice that social democracy supported the Government in this "war of defense." But Liebknecht soon broke over the hurdle. He blustered and burrowed, got behind the "localists" those anarchistic-socialistic laborers on the periphery of the Trade Unions, and got into touch with Rosa Luxemburg and all sorts of Russian revolutionary elements. Radek, under the pseudonym of Parabellum, published his incendiary articles in the *Berner Tagwacht* against the militaristic, traitorous, German social democracy. Bebel at once discovered that Radek was a rogue and kicked him out of the party. Liebknecht started a secret propaganda which kept the organization busy altering their position. Once in the Reichstag he rushed onto the podium wildly protesting against the "wholesale murder" and "war-loan swindle." An uproar was the result. Dr. Müller-Meiningen sprang up in greatest excitement — it almost came to blows when some one pulled him back from the platform. The president, decrepit, old, Herr Kaempf, rushed around in despair ringing his bell, which of course no one heard. He afterwards begged the press not to report the scandalous affair, so it was passed over in silence and the public heard nothing of it.

KARL LIEBKNECHT

The Spartacus letters appeared about the end of 1915. Gray, typewritten, on diverse topics — length according to desire. Flaming protests against the war, against the princes, against imperialistic social democracy, and inciting the proletariat to revolution. More than once one of these letters fell into my hands. Where they came from I do not know. They were signed — Spartacus. One laid them aside with a smile.

In the spring of 1915 the sheriff got hold of Liebknecht. As a representative he was immune, therefore he had to be taken in the act. One evening he distributed inflammatory circulars on Potsdamerplatz, crying out at the same time: "Down with the Government!" He was arrested, searched, etc. The court besought the Reichstag to allow them to institute criminal proceedings against him. And the Reichstag did so, although it was but a political offense he was charged with. Herr von Payer, speaker of the parties, explained their decision thus: "The fact that it does not concern the right of one single representative but that it concerns the right of the Reichstag, makes it necessary to investigate in such a case, whether the House and the general public have such a great interest in the coöperation of the member concerned that it may interfere with justice." The House disregarded all good traditions and acted politically very unwisely. For now the martyr's crown was placed on Liebknecht's head. He was sentenced to two years, six months, penitentiary; was not disenfranchised, however, because the court expressed the opinion that he was not actuated by dishonorable motives but that political fanaticism had been the mainspring of his actions. Inveighing against the reactionary or Alldeutsch press or the National Military Court was punishable with almost double the sentence and disenfranchisement.

Liebknecht entered the prison house: a new test. But still he remained unenlightened; things had already gone too far. Hate ate deeper and deeper; fanatic idealism became idiosyncrasy. His nerves went to pieces in the many, many hours of suffocating loneliness. Martyred and brooding, but one thing danced before his eyes: Down with the system! Give it the death-blow if the whole world goes down with it!

Prince Max's cabinet, with Secretary Scheidemann, presented him with freedom. Would he restrain himself now, give his nerves the rest they need? No, he sprang into the midst of political life once more. A new propaganda began and in a few days the revolution was there.

Liebknecht triumphed; this was his revolution — this was why he fought and suffered. On the first revolution night he slept in the bed of Wilhelm II. His thirst for revenge was slaked. Now he could help to build up the new Freedom. But when the cabinet was formed and he was invited to take part in it, he refused, went over to the left and organized the Spartacus spectacle—German Bolshevism. And what he planned was terror, what he saw was rage, what he spoke was chastisement, and what he screamed was blood.

A mixture of idealism, fanaticism, vanity, and psychosis. One would like to send for a nerve specialist.

In civil life he is, or was at least, an extraordinarily pleasant man who blushed like a schoolboy when spoken to. This day he fled like a hunted animal from one place to another. He never remained more than one or two days in the same hotel; an auto was ever ready at hand. Were the sheriffs really after him? When he staged the second revolution, when he, Ledebour, and Scholze established a Spartacist secondary Government and conjured up a week of blood for Berlin, Noske, his one-time party comrade, brought up artillery and infantry against them, and it became a struggle for life or death.

The uprising was put down. Liebknecht was conquered and surprised in secret conference with Rosa Luxemburg. They were arrested and taken to prison. The auto broke down and Liebknecht tried to escape. At least this is the story his military guards told. Three shots, and his body lay stretched on the ground.

But his fame will live after him — the fame of a herostratus.

XLIV

WALTER ADRIAN SCHÜCKING

Before the war, when one spoke of pacifism to otherwise well-educated people, they would regard one pityingly from the side and shrug their shoulders: " Another one who believes in a world peace. And he wants to be a practical politician, wants to be taken seriously! " That was the general view: exaggerated utopianism. This contemptuous rejection of a magnificent and practical political idea springs in ninety-nine cases out of a hundred from ignorance of what modern pacifism really means. One conjures up a blurred picture of a communistic paradise of universal peace, without any idea of how much practical work has really been done to create a political and international peace organization.

Whoever knows a little of history ought to know that this thought has been seeking expression for over two thousand years. At first it was the shimmering Fata Morgana of a universal kingdom which haunted the brains of men even as late as Napoleon III. Imperial Rome, in a frenzy of expansion, almost created a world empire. In the Middle Ages the Catholic Church represented this idea — the Kaisers were but executive officials of this Christian central organization. The Reformation dissolved the unity of the medieval world. The cabinet and coalition wars began; politicians and scholars agitated for a federation of States in order to bring about a permanent peace. From Campanella, Ernst II, the Landgraf von Hessen-Rheinfels, Sully, down to Saint Pierre and to Kant, who, in contrast to the monarchists, called upon the people themselves to form a federation of constitutional states.

The Napoleonic wars brought a wave of nationalism over Europe which still surges against the cliffs of a future peace. Only a few held fast to the great humanitarian thoughts of our forefathers of the eighteenth century during this nationalistic intoxication which took hold of almost the whole of German intelligence before the war. Most were ashamed to cherish just or noble thoughts in regard to internationalism, and where the borders ended they closed the Bible, the catechism, and the choral book, too. The mockery and contempt of society, where the tone was given by officers and assistant judges, was harder to bear than their own bad conscience when they acted against the dictates of their better feelings.

Whoever openly confessed being a pacifist was immediately branded a dreamer, an enthusiast, and an enemy of the nation in the eyes of all correct people, the *Täg-*

liche Rundschau and the *Deutsche Tageszeitung*,— he had no feeling for nationality, he must surely be a Jew. It was best not to associate with such people. Only a few firm characters were not to be challenged and made no concessions.

One such was Walter Schücking who knew what it was to swim against the current for fifteen years. He represented a part of the history of sufferings which pacifism underwent in Germany for many years, until through a horrible deluge of blood it came forth victorious.

The Schückings were all idealists, men who were true to themselves, who drove straight for the goal. They were men of ideas, of imagination, and yet they were practical thinkers and writers, too — Lewin Schücking, author and friend of Freiligraph and Frau Droste-Hülshoff, was Walter's grandfather, Luise von Gall, the novelist, his grandmother. He inherited his critical reasoning powers from his father, Lothar Schücking, director of a provincial court. And from his mother's side a bit of the oppositional democratic spirit of the old progressive party. At home they said he was the image of his grandfather, Heinrich Beitzke. Grandfather was a sturdy Progressive representative in the sixties, and the only man who had the courage to oppose single-handed the Bismarck-Roonsche military organization. He battled continually for the old Landwehr

WALTER ADRIAN SCHÜCKING

system, and was a sworn enemy of the militarizing of Prussia. In his history of the German war of independence, 1813–1815, he pays the highest tribute to the Prussian Landwehr.

Walter Schücking was born in Münster, 1875. A tall, slender, thoughtful man, a hard-headed, uncompromising Westphalian to whom conviction was everything. In personal relations one of the softest, most obliging of men, at times like a dreamy professor of the old type.

He attended the Pauliner gymnasium at Münster. His idealism and upright character showed itself early. While still a youth he refused to copy or sneak. The others regarded him somewhat askance for this. At the universities of Bonn, Munich, Berlin, and Göttingen he studied history, political and national science. As a student in the nineties he showed himself a modern idealist and was against the student's corps. There was an heirloom in the family, a copy of Hugo Grotius' *De Jure Belli ac Pacis,* which no one studied as diligently as Walter. For two hundred years it had been the custom for each member of the family to write his name on the title page of this book.

As the pupil of von Bar, professor of international law, he habilitated himself in Göttingen. His memorial on the "Seacoast and International Rights" won a prize. At the age of twenty-seven, after two years at

Breslau, he was called to Marburg as professor of national and international law. Althoff, the all-powerful minister of education, valued him highly. It seemed as if a quick rise was in store for Walter Schücking, but such was not the case.

He became democratic, national-socialistic, and independent. This was more than the Royal Prussian Ministerial Director could stand. Althoff told him one day that of course he could lecture on whatever he pleased, but whether the State would make use of him as a teacher was a different thing. This was the first box on the ear. He was done for in Marburg. When he became chairman of the Liberal Verein of Marburg, the other professors' wives made his wife calls of condolence and explained that it would probably be difficult for her to remain a member of their circle any longer. That was the way it looked a few years ago in the professors' republic. We needed a new writer of burlesques.

But it was no joke for Walter Schücking; his path of thorns was just beginning. He sank further and further in disfavor. When he publicly declared the Polish expropriation laws to be a national disgrace, he received a rebuke from the Minister of Education and for this reason was expelled from the legal examining committee.

For many years his pupils had the greatest difficulty

in getting ahead; Schücking was looked down upon everywhere. It was a fight in the dark, but he held out. How glad they would have been to be rid of him! While his scientific works were everywhere else recognized, the Marburg faculty considered him nothing but a "spoiler of our youth." Naturally under these circumstances his election for the Rectorship was not to be thought of. There was Professor Enneccerus, a miserable, old national chief, a ruffian who sought to hold Schücking under with brutal words. Schücking was a man of fine sensibilities and no doubt suffered under this treatment, but he overcame it all. Only his features acquired a trace of bitterness as time wore on. His worst enemies were the curators of the Marburg University. They were angry because this intellectually and politically infected man had the largest attendance of students. They instituted a disciplinary investigation against him on the ground of things they had heard over their beer mugs concerning his lectures. In the summer of 1911 one of these curators told him they would give him the desired one semester vacation for scientific research purposes if he would first go to the Minister of Education and tell him he had changed his political views.

And this when the war broke out! Schücking was one of the first to be put on the black list. The Eleventh Army Corps gave the order that he was not to publish any more of his international ideas or to express them even theoretically, and that all correspondence with foreign scholars was to cease. He could neither travel abroad nor anywhere near the German frontiers,— and this was a man of international reputation!

His connections were many and wide: Lammasch, Streit, Constant d'Estournelles, Sir Thomas Barclay, and James Brown Scott were but a few. In the meantime he had been appointed member of the Institut du Droit International. His works, *The Use of Mines in Sea Warfare, The Organization of the World, The Work Done at the Hague, The Hague League of Nations,* are rich with ideas and practical suggestions in regard to the most important problems of pacifism and internationalism. But it was war and every word in regard to an understanding was hated by the military authorities. Pacifism was looked upon as unlawful rivalry of the war business and was forbidden on that ground; it was almost wiped out. The under-officer commands, and the undesired thought has but to commit suicide.

His letters were opened; telegrams from abroad were held back for months. He was lucky to escape imprisonment. In the spring of 1915, with the aid of the Foreign Office, he was allowed to attend a conference at The Hague. When he returned he brought the Dutch Under-Secretary of State Dresselhuis' offer to act

WALTER ADRIAN SCHÜCKING

as peace intermediary. But he received the brusque order to telegraph Dresselhuis that he should stay at home.

Schücking's idea of organizing international relations on a pacific basis was fought for years by the very people who now defend his ideas the loudest. Now that the war was ended and even the greatest militarists were shrieking for a reconciliation, Schücking's time had come. He had passed the last station of suffering. His day had dawned. The Democrats elected him to the National Assembly. As the second speaker of the party he made a great speech with a compact conception of the whole which made a deep impression on the House. The Conservatives protested and the chauvinists barked.

The Government appointed him head of the committee for investigation of the treatment of war prisoners in Germany, and sent him to Versailles as peace delegate. As a logical pacifist he rejected the peace conditions dictated by the Entente.

The last shall be first, says the Bible. The shadows have departed from Schücking's path and he can strive openly toward his goal. That which lies behind was only a tormenting dream — the old, reactionary, petty, tradition-bound Prussia in the shape of a small university town.

Now he can breathe freely in the pure morning air and exercise mind and body at will.

XLV

GUSTAV NOSKE

Open your Roman history books. There you will find historical pictures which bear great resemblance to the unrest of the present Germany, still trembling from revolution and war. There are the same gloomy factors: the proletariat returning from long years of war, of butchery and murder, to reach out after the golden thrones of those who remained at home.

Marius, the farmer's son, had put down the African uprising, had freed Italy from the forbidding Cimbri and Teutons, and now returns home to Rome. His unoccupied army began to cry out for land, for property, for work. But the Conservatives, the nobles as well as the most radical, the idlers and scum of the Roman streets, protested against favoring the veterans, both from selfish motives. Both had to relinquish something: the nobles would have had to give up land, and the mob their political pampering and state support. Marius called his veterans into the city and politics were made with the club. Terror swept over Rome. The property owners began to cringe; even Marius seemed to shudder before the spirits he had conjured up. As a soldier and commander of the army, order

GUSTAV NOSKE

and discipline were everything to him. In this hour of hesitation the nobles approached him with hypocritical words, and when the next deed of violence endangered the Fatherland, as the Senate declared, he offered to put down the rising. His companions of yesterday were driven to the Capitol and before Marius could prevent it, they were stoned to death by the enraged noble youths with the tiles from their prison roof. Marius was done for completely. All the great reforms were ended before one step had been taken toward their realization.

Is Gustav Noske a Marius? I do not know. He has won no battles and planned no campaigns. But like Marius he has come up from the bottom, and his massive, rough strength lies in his energy. He is a tall, almost boorish fellow, and has spent twelve years as a snarling under-officer. He is a wood-chopper by profession, and a dissenter. His almost square head is covered with a stiff brush of dark brown hair which grows low over his forehead. A tremendous mustache shades his mouth. Gold-rimmed spectacles soften the rough features. Whenever he speaks in Parliament there is generally a surprise. He speaks roughly and clumsily but to the point; it is like a huge ax chopping down a tree, an intellectual wood-chopper. A man of will through and through, concentrated decision, cold-blooded strength and power, it is an unalloyed, esthetic joy to hear him dividing his rough-hewn chips between the Right and Left. If someone contradicts he is not disturbed, but goes quietly on with his square-built speech, neatly throwing in the answer.

Is the politician Noske fashioned in the same mould? Hardly. He is Prussian, born in the Mark — a proletarian who hungered his way to sturdy manhood, a fir tree which cannot quite become a pine in spite of its height, for the ground on which it grew was only the sandy soil of the Mark. He was a Social Democrat, an opposer, but he saw another and higher sort of human being in those who were not of the proletariat. He was not an equality enthusiast, nor a social fanatic who believed in August Bebel's thousand-year kingdom. He was a corporal of Social Democracy who reckoned with the realities of political life.

His career is quickly told. His father still sat at the weaving frame while Gustav went to the people's school and later to grammar school. Thereupon he became a wood-chopper and wandered to Halle, to Frankfurt am Main, and then to Liegnitz. Toward the end of the eighties, while Bismarck's socialistic laws were still in force, he entered the labor movement. In 1896 he became editor of the Social Democrat paper in his native city, Brandenburg. Two years later he was engaged in the same capacity at Königsberg in Prussia, and five years later he was editor-in-chief of the *Volksstimme*

GUSTAV NOSKE

in Chemnitz. Since the beginning of the century he has been city councillor in East Prussia as well as in Saxony. He entered the Reichstag in 1906, during the colonial rumpus when Bülow broke with the Center and dissolved the session.

In the Reichstag he held fast to the right wing of the party and was soon the army and navy specialist. His book on *Colonial Policy and Social Democracy* appeared later, in 1914. He seemed to be the right person for the army budget, was sent to the commission, and finally became assistant reporter. This was no small affair. He was petted and pampered by the military. The most secret things were whispered in his ear. He saw the storm clouds gathering over Germany; secret sittings began to increase. Noske participated in everything year in and year out, even Tirpitz's naval policy, in his blind love for the navy. 1914, 1915, 1916, 1917, 1918. Noske's faith is not to be shaken. He believes in German militarism without approving of an all too conspicuous development.

In October, 1918, things began to stir on the water front. It had been expected earlier in the month but only broke on the twenty-eighth. Officers had called for men for a last stand against England. This was the match in the powder barrel. Three times they prevented the vessels from putting out to sea. The crews mutinied. Officers were dismissed. A battle of everybody against everybody else threatened to break out in the harbor. Finally the third squadron steamed toward Kiel. The chief hoped to ward off the worst by this maneuver. Many got a furlough on land. "They could wear off their spirits in pleasures." A mob collected in the streets and marched to the Union house. There was a meeting, political debates, but no one thought of a revolution. The day passed quietly — it was the first of November. On Saturday the sailors found the Union house closed. The few had grown to six hundred. Excitement prevailed. Fire begins to gleam under the ashes. Sunday comes. Two hundred condemned sailors from the *Markgraf* are to be brought on land and taken to prison. When they were to be set on land one of the guards refused to do his duty. All but a very few declared themselves on his side, but the delinquents were unloaded somehow. In the meantime the Union was set in motion. They were mostly Independent Social Democrats. Circulars were distributed; the stone began to roll. In the evening ten thousand marched to the prison and freed the condemned sailors. There was a conflict with the soldiers. Eight dead remained on the pavement. The Governor of Kiel and leaders of the Social Democratic party begged the Government in Berlin to send a cabinet member. The Berlin press was not allowed to report what took place. "Harmless street fight. A few dead. Of no importance."

GUSTAV NOSKE

The air was growing sultry. Revolution began to show its head. The Governor negotiated with a deputation of sailors. On both sides courtesy and obligingness. In the meantime Noske and Secretary Haussmann arrived at Kiel. Noske was wholly unknown there, but he soon got into touch with the people. His one idea was to create order as soon as possible and allay the excitement. He had no idea what was under way and what would spread like wildfire over the whole nation. Regular negotiations began; anxious hours passed. On the 6th of November Noske advised the sailors to be reasonable. The day after the whole scene had changed. Revolution took the country by storm. Only Berlin was quiet. Noske was made Governor of Kiel. Within a few hours he issued his first mandate: " The food is to be uniform. . . . Sailors are no longer to be addressed in the third person."

On the 9th of November, as Ebert took the portfolio from the hands of Prince Max, Noske already felt himself an official revolutionist. It was up to him to create order in Berlin.

Weeks passed by; the Independents in the cabinet began to murmur. Haase, Dittmann, and Barth resigned. The first unrest flared up in Berlin. The People's marine division rebelled. The Christmas battle for the possession of the palace began. The majority Socialists took the places of the departing Independents.

Noske was one of these. He was looked upon as a strong man. Ledebour, Liebknecht, Eichhorn, and Scholz were secretly preparing a Spartacist insurrection. The second revolution began. But Noske was not yet ready. Hours and days of tension followed. The majority Social Democrat organization patrolled the streets for days in order to protect the Ebert-Scheidemann Government.

Finally Noske was ready. Hoffmann, the General of Brest-Litowsk fame, was his silent Chief of the Staff for the retaking of Berlin. The city was surrounded; Government troops marched in from all sides. The buildings occupied by the Spartacists were recaptured. Hand grenades and machine guns were at work — Berlin was a bloody battle field.

Noske triumphed, the victory was his. A Hindenburg of the proletariat? Or a Ludendorff of the "upper" circles?

At the National Assembly it was a matter of course that Noske was to be the new Minister of War. His was the task of building up a new army. Compulsory service was not yet done away with by law. But in reality it was a thing of the past. Two new army and navy bills were put through in double-quick time. The wild volunteer system with all its usual methods of advertisement was instituted in its place. A modest territorial army was recruited: one hundred and fifty marks with five marks extra a day, free board and uniform. Military service soon became a lucrative business.

The third revolution was approaching. Everywhere strikes were blazing up, the Communists at the front, the Independents not far behind in order not to lose their contact with the radical masses. "What has the Government done to fulfill the promises of the Social Revolution?" they asked. "Nothing! No socializing! No councils!" The storm broke. A new Noske campaign began. The seething Rühr Revier was again taken. Halle was cleaned out and in Berlin savage street fighting raged for days. Murder and death were the watchwords. Barricades were stormed, houses demolished. Human beings fell like flies. The Furies of War grew hysterical. The mob began to plunder. Vagabonds and ruffians violated the lives and property of others. Noske drove in with a heavy fist. He led a second battle of Tannenberg. No quarter. Wreathe the laurel about his brow, ye citizens, ye who sat trembling behind your stoves.

If it were only not for the epilogue: with militaristic snap and go the Government troops court-martialed and shot on the slightest provocation; there were painful incidents without substantial justification. Noske had put Berlin under martial law and threatened death to everyone caught with a weapon in his hands. If it had only stopped at this! But inferior officers and leaders immediately took things into their own hands, and many an innocent victim was the result.

There were sharp conflicts between Noske and Haase at the National Assembly on this account. These were not mere wordy duels with pistol and sword; they were a battle of hand grenades. "Liars and assassinators!" shouted the extreme left. "There are plain everyday dogs, and there are swine, bloodhounds, and Noske dogs," proclaimed the circulars. And Noske screamed in savage excitement from the Parliament tribune: "I enter a complaint against all incendiaries, and that is what Herr Haase and all his friends are. The blood that has been spilled be on your own heads!"

In answer to Haase's accusation that he had overstepped his rights, Noske said: "In such dangerous situations it is not paragraphs that count, but results!"

This was the proclamation of war, "Might before Right." This was the speech of a condottiere: thesis and antithesis. Remember Marius!